THE *30-Minute*
LOW-CARB
COOKBOOK

THE 30-Minute
LOW-CARB
COOKBOOK

100
Simple & Satisfying Recipes
for a Healthy Diet

PAMELA ELLGEN

ROCKRIDGE
PRESS

Interior and Cover Designer: Antonio Valverde
Photo Art Director/Art Manager: Sara Feinstein
Editor: Bridget Fitzgerald
Production Editor: Ashley Polikoff
Photography: Darren Muir

ISBN: Print 978-1-64152-507-7
eBook: 978-1-64152-508-4

For everyone who
embarks on a
healthier lifestyle–

you can do this!

Contents

Introduction

I CAME TO A LOW-CARB DIET BY WAY OF THE DESSERT BUFFET. It was my freshman year of college, and I had never seen so many delicious foods all in one place. My mom had raised me on a quintessential healthy diet that looked like a textbook example of the USDA MyPlate—protein, vegetables, fruit, and grains. In her kitchen and with our family's active lifestyle, maintaining a healthy, slender physique was easy.

But in the college cafeteria, all bets were off—waffles smothered in peanut butter, bananas, and syrup for breakfast, endless pasta and breadsticks for lunch, and six flavors of ice cream on deck every night. No surprise, I quickly packed on the "freshman 15" and then some. During my sophomore year, I saw a photo of myself and cringed. What had happened?

I didn't know anything about nutrition, clearly, but I figured I'd cut back to just one dessert a day. Then I decided to skip my morning scone. I made myself choose between Cajun waffle fries and the cookies-and-cream milk shakes I had ploughed through during late-night study sessions. They weren't exactly extreme measures, but they were enough to send the scale in the other direction.

You see, even small changes to your carb intake can make a difference. You can achieve small victories if you reduce the number of carbs—especially the refined ones—in your diet. Replace one burger bun with a lettuce wrap. Swap your blended coffee drink for a cold-brew coffee over ice. Forgo the French fries in favor of roasted broccoli.

To me, a successful approach is one that you will be able to follow not just for 30 days, but for life. Sustainability is what matters in the long term—for both your waistline and your overall health. It has been shown that reducing your carb intake not only helps with weight loss, but also mitigates other cardiovascular risk factors: lowering elevated blood glucose, insulin, and triglycerides, reducing small dense LDL particles ("bad" cholesterol) and glycated hemoglobin (HbA1c) levels (a measure of your risk for diabetes), lowering blood pressure while increasing HDL ("good" cholesterol) levels, and in some cases reversing nonalcoholic fatty liver disease.

In plain English, a low-carb diet may help reduce your risk factors for several of the most common and dangerous health conditions: diabetes, heart disease, high cholesterol, and high blood pressure.

If you're struggling with any of these health conditions, seeking to lose a few pounds, or simply want to add a few more healthy recipes to your rotation, I want you to be able to do so in a way that is easy and convenient. That's why the recipes in this book can all be prepared within 30 minutes, including prep time. This way, you can easily adopt a low-carb diet without taking on a part-time job in your kitchen. I've chosen recipes that have accessible ingredients, are easy to prepare, and taste really good!

Over the past five years, I have written more than a dozen cookbooks, including several on the low-carb lifestyle. My hope is that in this book you'll discover that a low-carb diet can be flavorful, sustainable, and help you achieve your health goals. Whether you overhaul your diet to keep your carbs under a daily threshold, or you simply replace a handful of your meals with lower-carb options, I know you're going to find tasty dishes that you'll enjoy for years to come. Let's get cooking!

THE LOW-CARB LIFE

One reason the low-carb diet is so popular is that for a lot of people it really works. It feels almost magical—you can eat as much as you need to feel satiated and lose weight without ever feeling hungry; your blood work and other health markers improve; and you can continue to eat most of the foods you already enjoy. Here are some of the benefits of the low-carb diet and how to make it work for you.

Advantages

Unlike more restrictive diets that involve weighing and measuring foods, stuffing ingredients into color-coded boxes, eliminating entire food groups, or living with chronic hunger, the low-carb diet is surprisingly freeing. There's only one thing to count—carbs—and you really can eat almost anything on a low-carb plan as long as you keep your carbs under a certain daily threshold.

In this book, recipes have about 20 grams of net carbs or fewer per serving, making it easy for you to keep your net carbs below 100 grams a day. "Net carbs" is simply the total number of carbs in grams minus the number of grams of fiber, so net carbs will be lower than total carbs in any recipe that contains fiber. The reason for this is that fiber has a positive effect on blood sugar, stabilizing it and slowing the effect of carbohydrates on blood glucose levels. Fiber has many other health benefits, including reducing the risk of colon cancer, improving heart health, and providing a more diverse gut microbiome. All that is to say the best bet is to look at net carbs when evaluating a recipe—any fiber is a good thing!

While you might be inclined to think that if reducing some carb intake is good, eliminating it altogether is better, this is short-sighted. Anything below 50 grams a day is sufficient to get you into ketosis, which is when your body turns fat into ketone bodies and burns that for fuel instead of glucose. (You're actually in a mild state of ketosis when you wake up in the morning.) Some diets may advocate for restricting your carb intake to less than 50 grams at all times, and sure, you might lose a lot of weight really quickly, but you're also much more likely to fall off the wagon. Additionally, the no-carb approach eliminates many healthy foods and nutrients from your diet, such as vegetables and fiber. It might appear helpful in the short term for weight loss, but a sustainable, long-term approach will include a greater variety of micronutrients that come from plant-based foods and some carbs. A low-carb diet that incorporates between 50 and 100 grams of net carbs a day is easier to follow while supporting your health goals (and you'll still get plenty of bright, colorful, and tasty vegetables on your plate).

Adaptations

A low-carb diet can take many forms. You can jump with both feet into a diet with roughly 50 to 60 grams of net carbs per day, or you can ease in and replace one high-carb meal or snack at a time. Neither approach is wrong. The more aggressive approach will involve more dramatic changes, both positive and negative. You're likely to lose weight more quickly, but you're also more likely to experience some side effects, such as headaches, lethargy, bad breath, and the infamous "Atkins attitude" (read: straight-up grouchy) that so many experience in the first week of going low-carb. A gradual approach will yield more subtle but perhaps more sustainable changes. Ultimately, choose the approach that works for you.

Low-Carb Versus Paleo or Keto

At first glance, a low-carb diet may look a lot like other popular diets that avoid carbs, such as the Paleo, keto, and Atkins diets. While they have one obvious similarity—reduced carbs—they have several key differences.

→ **PALEO** Popularized by Loren Cordain, the Paleo diet starts with the premise that humans should eat the foods that were available to our hunter-gatherer ancestors before the agricultural revolution. The diet forbids sugar, grains, legumes, potatoes, dairy, and refined vegetable oils. As the diet has become more mainstream, variations, such as the primal diet, may include dairy and unrefined sugars such as maple syrup and honey. The result is a diet that's naturally lower in carbs than the standard American diet. But because fruit, nuts, and other starchy root vegetables, such as sweet potatoes, are still plentiful on the menu, you can easily eat more than 100 grams of total carbs per day on a Paleo diet. Additionally, fat content may vary wildly depending on whether you eat organ and fatty cuts of meats, as some Paleo proponents recommend, or stick with Cordain's low-fat and low-carb approach.

→ **KETO** The keto diet is a low-carb and high-fat diet. While it has no specific foods that are off-limits, they must fit within the stringent guidelines of a diet that's roughly 70 to 80 percent fat, 20 percent protein, and 5 to 10 percent (or less) total carbohydrates. The diet strives to put the body into a state of ketosis, in which fat is burned for fuel instead of carbohydrates, and the body manufactures ketone bodies (water-soluble compounds made by the liver from fatty acids) that can be used in the absence of glucose. The keto diet necessarily involves an adaptation period that may be unpleasant, often referred to

Whatever approach you choose, the low-carb diet is easy to implement in the kitchen because you probably already cook with many of the common low-carb foods, such as chicken, steak, eggs, cheese, and vegetables. In fact, you and your family may not even notice much of a difference in how your meals look on your plates because they're filled with familiar foods!

Results

If you're looking to lose weight, a low-carb diet succeeds for two primary reasons: It reduces hunger and consequently total calorie intake, and it mobilizes fat stores to fuel energy needs.

as the "keto flu." Potential benefits of the diet are rapid weight loss without hunger, mental clarity, and according to some, reversal of some chronic health conditions.

→ **ATKINS** Similar to the keto diet, the Atkins diet is a low-carb and high-fat diet. It has evolved from its original plan, which included only protein, fat, cheese, nuts, seeds, and a handful of nonstarchy, low-carb vegetables that added up to only 25 grams of daily net carbs. Now it includes a phased plan that gradually increases net carbs from 25 grams to up to 100 grams daily. Additionally, the diet now recommends eating 12 to 15 grams of net carbs from "foundation vegetables," such as arugula, spinach, mushrooms, celery, zucchini, green beans, or any nonstarchy vegetable, which was not a requirement in earlier iterations. It also discourages processed foods unless they're official Atkins products.

→ **LOW-CARB** A low-carb diet means different things to different people. In this book, it means avoiding starches, sweeteners, and most fruits. The recipes in this book sometimes fall within the parameters of the other diets. They are designed not only to be low in carbohydrates, but also to be healthy. There's no need to slather your baked chicken with butter or top your steak with slabs of bacon just to make them fit certain ratios. Sure, butter and bacon have their place, but they're not essential to seeing success when cutting carbs. This book is about cooking healthy, (mostly) whole foods that are naturally low in carbohydrates.

All in all, every body is different, and each person will find success with a different dietary plan. I prefer low-carb over more restrictive diets because I find it to be more sustainable—the opportunity is right there in your kitchen to live a lower-carb lifestyle and achieve whatever your health goals may be.

Your body's primary source of energy is glucose. You can get that glucose either from consuming carbohydrates or from converting fat (either fat you eat or fat you carry on your body) to a useable form of energy, a process called gluconeogenesis. This process is at work every single day in your body. In fact, it's essential to your survival; it's the reason you don't suffer from excessively low blood glucose levels at night while you're sleeping.

A low-carb diet mimics this fasting state because it isn't supplying that steady stream of glucose, and your body is forced to convert stored body fat into useable energy. Hence, you don't experience blood sugar crashes, and you don't feel particularly hungry on a low-carb diet. If you're one of the many people who doesn't feel hungry when you first wake up, this is exactly the type of feeling a low-carb diet provides—but all the time!

Here's the trick, though: Initially the low-carb diet is enough to generate weight loss without counting calories because you naturally eat fewer calories thanks to feeling less hungry. However, long-term studies (greater than 24 months) show that eventually weight loss stalls on a low-carb diet. A possible explanation for this is that if your diet supplies all the energy you need to function through the fat in your diet, there's no need for your body to burn stored body fat. To lose more weight, you actually have to drop your calories further. At this point, a more structured approach (yes, counting the other macronutrients and total calories) might be helpful. That's why I have provided the nutrition facts for all the recipes in the book. If you're just starting out, you don't need to worry about the numbers too much—everything in the book is healthy and low-carb—but as you fine-tune things, the numbers will be there for you!

THE LOW-CARB KITCHEN

One of the biggest things you can do to ensure your long-term success on a low-carb diet is to stock your kitchen with wholesome, hearty ingredients that enable you to whip up healthy meals (and snacks!) in minutes. Unlike diets that rely on processed foods, the low-carb diet involves plenty of fresh foods, so you may find that you're hitting the grocery store more often to grab a steak or some fresh vegetables. That said, there are a few things you can keep in your refrigerator and pantry to make meal times easy.

The Basics

Here are 10 items that will have you well on your way to making many of the recipes in this book.

→ **Olive oil and coconut oil:** If you've been on a low-fat diet for any length of time, you're in for some good news: Oils such as olive oil and coconut oil are back on the menu. Olive oil is used in salad dressings and other raw dishes, as well as some stovetop cooking. Coconut oil is used for oven-roasted foods and is also a staple in desserts. If you like the strong aroma and flavor of coconut oil, you can choose an unrefined, virgin coconut oil. Otherwise, refined and deodorized versions may be a good way to introduce this cooking fat into your diet.

→ **Nuts and nut butters:** Almonds, peanuts, macadamia nuts, pecans, and the nut butters made from them are used in many low-carb recipes. Almonds and peanuts are roughly 77 percent fat, with the remainder equal parts carbs and protein. Macadamia nuts and pecans are about 93 percent fat. Cashews are slightly higher in carbs but may be included in your low-carb diet at your discretion.

→ **Coconut milk:** Use this creamy, delicious liquid to flavor soups, curries, and sauces. It is about 94 percent fat and 5 percent carbs and has roughly 30 percent fewer calories than heavy cream. Because it is plant-based, it also offers a host of other phytonutrients and antioxidants.

→ **Avocados:** Avocados are a great way to add healthy, satisfying fats to your diet without upping your carb count dramatically. If you notice that they ripen before you're ready to use them, simply pop them into the refrigerator to slow down the process by a few days. If you need even more time, cut the avocados in half, remove the pit, and scoop out the flesh. Place them on a baking sheet lined with parchment paper, and freeze until solid. Defrost and use in smoothies, salad dressings, or guacamole.

→ **Lemons and limes:** For a lot of flavor and minimal calories and carbohydrates, citrus fruits such as lemons and limes are my go-to. Please don't use bottled juice; it will compromise the flavor of your dish.

→ **Red-wine and white-wine vinegars:** As illustrated so beautifully in the book *Salt, Fat, Acid, Heat* by chef and author Samin Nosrat, acid is an essential component in almost every dish. Just a few drops can brighten any recipe. Bonus: A double-blind, placebo-controlled study done in Japan showed that eating just a tablespoon of vinegar per day can reduce body weight, waist circumference, and triglycerides.

→ **Sea salt:** You probably already have table salt in your kitchen, but sea salt is important for a few reasons. First, it contains less sodium per teaspoon than table salt, so you're less likely to oversalt things. Also, because it isn't iodized, it's less likely to impart a metallic flavor to your food. Finally, it contains trace minerals that are important as you lose water weight on a low-carb diet.

→ **Basic spices:** Cumin, smoked paprika, cinnamon, chili powder, and black pepper are essential savory spices that are used throughout this book. They impart flavor without adding carbohydrates or calories to the finished dish. They also have a long shelf life. I like to use them in most of my savory recipes, especially those from cuisines around the globe.

→ **Eggs:** Nothing cooks faster than eggs, and they can be your go-to when hunger strikes. They are roughly 70 percent fat and 30 percent protein. Ideally, choose pasture-raised eggs for the best nutrition and animal welfare.

→ **Chicken thighs:** Because a low-carb diet embraces fat, chicken thighs are as welcome at the dinner table as chicken breasts. Boneless, skinless chicken thighs are roughly 70 percent protein and 30 percent fat.

The Upgrades

Here are a handful of other ingredients that I use frequently in cooking and are helpful, but not essential, to have on hand.

→ **Low-sodium soy sauce:** Choose a gluten-free soy sauce if you follow a gluten-free diet.

→ **Sambal oelek chili paste:** This is great for spicing up nearly anything without needing to cut into a fresh pepper. It's an Indonesian chili paste made from red chiles, salt, and vinegar. Find it in the Asian foods section of many grocery stores, at Asian markets, or online. A good substitute is chili garlic sauce, such as ones by the Huy Fong brand, or a pinch of crushed red pepper flakes.

→ **Canned tomatoes:** Tomatoes are almost entirely made up of carbohydrates, but they still have a place in a low-carb diet and are used in limited quantities in many different recipes.

→ **Fresh herbs:** If you have the space, even a window box with fresh mint, basil, thyme, oregano, and rosemary will do wonders for your cooking.

The Swaps

Many traditional carbohydrate-rich foods can easily be replaced with low-carb versions. I won't try to convince you that cauliflower rice tastes the same as white rice, but it's better than a bare bowl under your stir-fry! Here are some of my faves.

→ **Spaghetti squash:** Cut spaghetti squash into rings, and remove the seeds and strings. Bake in the oven (see page 28), then scrape out the flesh with a fork to yield a pasta-like texture.

→ **Zucchini:** This low-carb summer vegetable makes a nice stand-in for pasta. Run it through a spiralizer if you have one, or use a vegetable peeler to create faux-fettuccine.

→ **Cauliflower:** Cauliflower is the go-to low-carb ingredient. You can steam it and mash it with a bit of butter and milk to make a nice substitute for mashed potatoes. Alternatively, grate it with a food processor to make cauliflower rice.

→ **Almond flour:** This can be used as breading for meat or in baking. It derives roughly 12 percent of its calories from carbohydrates instead of the nearly 90 percent found in all-purpose flour. Almond flour is made from blanched almonds and may be labeled as blanched almond flour. The designation differentiates it from almond meal, which comes from unblanched, skin-on almonds.

The Tools

Here are the seven essential pieces of cooking equipment for your kitchen. Certainly you'll need some others, but these are the items I use every day.

→ **Chef's knife:** A good chef's knife is the primary knife I use in my kitchen to chop vegetables, trim meats, and do much of my other cutting. Invest in a good-quality knife (and a wood or bamboo cutting board), and have it sharpened regularly. It should feel somewhat heavy in your hand and not have any teeth on the blade.

→ **Sauté pan:** A heavy-bottomed 12-inch sauté pan can last a lifetime. Choose stainless steel or copper; avoid nonstick pans when possible. A cast-iron skillet is also an excellent option and can be transferred from stovetop to oven.

→ **Rimmed baking sheet:** Also known as a half sheet pan, a rimmed baking sheet is perfect for roasting vegetables and meats and allows for maximum airflow and browning.

→ **Saucepan:** Choose at least a four-quart saucepan with a lid. It is good for making soups and stews, steaming vegetables, and making sauces.

→ **Baking dish:** A two- to four-quart glass or ceramic baking dish is essential for cooking casseroles, braised meats, and other baked dishes.

→ **Food processor:** A small (two-cup) or large (six- to eight-cup) food processor makes prep work easy. It can chop, grate, and slice vegetables and nuts, and it works well for making creamy dishes, such as soups and cauliflower mash, especially if you don't have a blender.

→ **Blender:** A countertop blender or a handheld immersion blender is useful for puréeing smoothies, soups, and sauces.

The Good, the Bad, and the Ugly on Sugar Substitutes

Research on artificial sweeteners such as sucralose, saccharin, and aspartame (Sweet'N Low, Equal, etc.) has consistently found that they may contribute to insulin resistance and obesity, disrupt the gut microbiome, increase overall calorie consumption, and reduce satiety. This is bad news if you're pounding diet sodas and Crystal Light like it's 1987. And it might also explain why you're still not losing weight while eating artificially sweetened foods. A 2017 study published in the *International Journal of Obesity* found that study participants who consumed artificially sweetened beverages replaced all of the calories they "saved" at subsequent meals.

Fortunately, there are some natural non-nutritive (meaning they don't contribute any calories) sweeteners, such as Swerve, stevia, and monk fruit, that are safe and effective sugar replacements. They may also have health benefits. According to research published in 2016 in the journal *Current Pharmaceutical Design*, stevia possesses therapeutic effects against several diseases, including cancer, diabetes, hypertension, inflammation, and obesity.

30-MINUTE MEALS

One of the perceived barriers to eating healthfully is that cooking takes too long, dirties too many dishes, and won't taste as good as food you can get in a restaurant. But that couldn't be further from the truth! I have found that limiting myself to just a handful of ingredients or only one pan can actually improve recipes and pushes me to be more creative and resourceful in the kitchen.

Cooking Hacks

To me, to hack a process means to ignore the conventional way of doing something and just think about what might make it easier, more efficient, or more flavorful—sometimes that means returning to a traditional technique that's often overlooked. Here are my top five low-carb cooking hacks.

→ **Make a pan sauce.** There's so much flavor in that pan after you've seared a steak or any other piece of meat or fish. Put it to good use by deglazing the pan with a splash of wine or broth. Scrape up the browned bits from the pan, and reduce the liquid until it's thick and syrupy, then pour it over the finished dish. Bonus: Cleanup is even easier.

→ **Use parchment paper to line your pan.** Lining your baking sheet with parchment paper before roasting vegetables or meat will make cleanup easier and allow you to use less cooking oil to keep food from sticking.

→ **Wash and prep on grocery day.** When you get home from the grocery store, instead of putting your food straight into the refrigerator, do yourself a favor by washing and preparing some or all of it. For example, gently wash lettuces and other sturdy leafy greens. Wrap them in paper towels and store in a sealed container. Now salads are even easier (and you didn't have to waste plastic packaging for the convenience of pre-washed lettuce!).

→ **Blanch it all.** Blanching vegetables simply means cooking them in a pot of boiling salted water until they're barely tender and brightly colored, then plunging them into ice water or running them under cool water to stop the cooking. To save time and hassle, prepare a week's worth of vegetables this way, beginning with the ones with the mildest flavor and moving on to those with a more assertive flavor. Store them in the refrigerator in sealed containers.

→ **Grill another batch.** After preparing one meal on the charcoal or gas grill, why not add another protein or vegetable to the grill to make use of the residual heat and enjoy all of the flavors grilling imparts?

About the Recipes

My goal with this book is to solve the common challenges of creating healthy meals quickly and easily. I'll offer solutions for meals using fresh, healthy ingredients and simple but timeless cooking techniques to create unforgettable flavors. Each recipe can, of course, be made in 30 minutes or less, from prep to table. To save you even more time, I'll suggest healthy store-bought products and cooking hacks whenever possible. The recipes also include labels (such as gluten-free, soy-free, vegetarian, vegan, dairy-free, and nut-free) for dietary considerations and tips to make them even more user-friendly. Tips may contain information on substituting or selecting ingredients, helpful cooking or prepping tips, variations on the dish to mix things up a little, and the best ways to store or repurpose any leftovers.

Spanakopita Frittata, page 13

1

breakfast and brunch

Peanut Butter Chocolate Protein Shake

GLUTEN-FREE, SOY-FREE, VEGETARIAN

Serves 1 | **PREP TIME:** 2 minutes

Protein shakes are a perennial favorite because they're easy to make and even easier to enjoy. I make a version of this shake nearly every day and appreciate the way it keeps me feeling full and energized until lunchtime.

1 cup whole milk or
    unsweetened
    plant-based milk

1 cup ice cubes

2 tablespoons natural
    peanut butter

1 scoop chocolate
    protein powder

Put the milk, ice, peanut butter, and protein powder in a blender, and blend until smooth, scraping down the sides as needed.

INGREDIENT TIP: Try to choose a protein powder with 20 to 30 grams of protein per serving and no added sugar. Most are sweetened with stevia or another non-nutritive sweetener. My favorite protein powder is Garden of Life Sport Organic Plant-Based Protein, chocolate flavor.

PER SERVING
Calories: 389;
Fat: 25g;
Saturated Fat: 9g;
Sodium: 325mg;
Total Carbohydrates: 19g;
Net Carbohydrates: 17g;
Fiber: 2g;
Sugar: 17g;
Protein: 26g

Creamy Dreamy Green Smoothie

DAIRY-FREE, GLUTEN-FREE, SOY-FREE, VEGAN

Serves 1 | **PREP TIME:** 2 minutes

The antioxidants, vitamins, and minerals in this smoothie make a healthy way to start your day. Antioxidants are found primarily in plants, and they combat oxidative stress in your body (think of it like rust forming on a car), thereby helping to keep you looking and feeling your best.

1 small avocado, pitted, peeled, and diced

1 lime, peeled

1 cup spinach

1 cup unsweetened almond milk

1 cup ice cubes

1 tablespoon almond butter

2 or 3 drops liquid stevia

Put the avocado, lime, spinach, almond milk, ice, almond butter, and liquid stevia in a blender, and blend until smooth, scraping down the sides as needed.

INGREDIENT TIP: To keep avocados fresher longer, cut them in half, remove the pit, and scoop out the flesh. Cut it into pieces, place on a parchment-lined baking sheet, and freeze until solid. Then transfer to a zip-top plastic freezer bag.

PER SERVING
Calories: 454;
Fat: 39g;
Saturated Fat: 5g;
Sodium: 220mg;
Total Carbohydrates: 28g;
Net Carbohydrates: 11g;
Fiber: 17g;
Sugar: 3g;
Protein: 9g

Blueberry-Flax Yogurt Parfait

GLUTEN-FREE, SOY-FREE, VEGETARIAN

Serves 1 | **PREP TIME:** 5 minutes

The probiotics in yogurt—whether dairy yogurt or a plant-based variety—add to the good bacteria in your gut. This improves digestion, aids in weight loss, increases energy, and even brightens your mood. That's a lot for some teeny little bacteria!

½ cup whole-milk plain yogurt

1 tablespoon ground flax meal

2 to 3 teaspoons liquid stevia

1 teaspoon extra-virgin olive oil

¼ teaspoon lemon zest

2 or 3 drops freshly squeezed
   lemon juice

¼ cup fresh blueberries

2 tablespoons chopped
   toasted pecans

1. Put the yogurt in a small bowl.
2. Stir in the flax meal, liquid stevia, olive oil, lemon zest, and lemon juice.
3. Top with the blueberries and pecans.

SUBSTITUTION TIP: To make this plant-based, choose a plain cashew- or coconut-based yogurt. My favorite is the full-fat variety of Forager.

PER SERVING
Calories: 367;
Fat: 31g;
Saturated Fat: 5g;
Sodium: 58mg;
Total Carbohydrates: 22g;
Net Carbohydrates: 10g;
Fiber: 12g;
Sugar: 6g;
Protein: 13g

Salted Peanut Butter and Chocolate Yogurt Cup

GLUTEN-FREE, SOY-FREE, VEGETARIAN

Serves 1 | **PREP TIME:** 5 minutes

Can you tell I love the combination of peanut butter and chocolate? I make no apologies—when you're transitioning to a low-carb diet, delicious and familiar flavor combinations make it much easier to stick with the plan.

½ cup whole-milk plain yogurt

2 or 3 drops liquid stevia

2 tablespoons creamy natural peanut butter

1 tablespoon no-sugar-added chocolate chips

Pinch flaky sea salt

1 tablespoon coarsely chopped salted peanuts

PER SERVING
Calories: 315;
Fat: 25g;
Saturated Fat: 7g;
Sodium: 439mg;
Total Carbohydrates: 18g;
Net Carbohydrates: 15g;
Fiber: 3g;
Sugar: 9g;
Protein: 15g

1. Put the yogurt in a small bowl.
2. Stir in the liquid stevia.
3. Add the peanut butter and chocolate chips, and stir until partly combined.
4. Top with the salt and peanuts.

VARIATION TIP: This works equally well with other nut butters, such as hazelnut or almond butter.

Crunchy Nut and Seed Granola

DAIRY-FREE, GLUTEN-FREE, SOY-FREE, VEGAN

Makes 6 cups (12 ½-cup servings) | **PREP TIME:** 5 minutes | **COOK TIME:** 25 minutes

Most granola recipes are loaded with sugar; in fact, if you look at the nutrition facts, you might mistake some for dessert! This version is built around filling protein and healthy fats, with a hint of sweetness from stevia. It includes pepitas (shelled pumpkin seeds), too. Don't fear the applesauce in this recipe! It adds only 1 gram of carbohydrate per serving and brings a nice bit of sweet and tart to the granola. Serve this over yogurt or with a splash of milk and a handful of berries for a delicious low-carb breakfast.

1 cup raw unsalted pecans

1 cup raw unsalted almonds

1 cup raw unsalted sunflower seeds

2 cups unsweetened coconut flakes

1 cup raw unsalted pepitas

¼ cup sesame seeds

2 teaspoons ground cinnamon

½ cup coconut oil

½ cup unsweetened applesauce

1 teaspoon pure vanilla extract

5 or 6 drops liquid stevia

**PER SERVING
(½ CUP)**
Calories: 399;
Fat: 38g;
Saturated Fat: 18g;
Sodium: 9mg;
Total Carbohydrates: 11g;
Net Carbohydrates: 5g;
Fiber: 6g;
Sugar: 3g;
Protein: 8g

1. Preheat the oven to 325°F. Line a rimmed baking sheet with parchment paper.

2. Put the pecans, almonds, and sunflower seeds in a food processor, and pulse until coarsely ground.

3. Add the coconut flakes, pepitas, sesame seeds, and cinnamon, and pulse once or twice, or until just combined.

4. In a medium bowl, whisk the coconut oil, applesauce, vanilla, and liquid stevia, then pour into the food processor, and pulse once or twice again until just combined.

5. Spread the mixture onto the baking sheet, transfer to the oven, and bake for 10 minutes.

6. Stir, then return the baking sheet to the oven, and bake for another 10 minutes.

7. Stir, then flatten with the back of a spatula, as if you're making dessert bars. Bake for a final 5 minutes, or until the mixture is golden brown and somewhat dried out.

LEFTOVERS: Allow the mixture to cool completely before storing. This will help the granola form crisp chunks. Store for up to one month in an airtight container.

Classic Pancakes

GLUTEN-FREE, SOY-FREE, VEGETARIAN

Serves 4 | **PREP TIME:** 5 minutes | **COOK TIME:** 15 minutes

There's something so nostalgic and comforting about pancakes. The only problem is that most are about as nutritious as a pastry—just simple starches that send you on a blood sugar roller coaster. These protein-rich pancakes have staying power and will keep you satisfied long after breakfast has ended. Top them with a handful of smashed fresh berries or a tablespoon of peanut butter.

3 large eggs

1 cup almond flour

½ cup whole milk

6 tablespoons melted
  butter, divided

2 tablespoons coconut flour

1 teaspoon pure vanilla extract

½ teaspoon ground cinnamon

½ teaspoon baking soda

½ teaspoon sea salt

PER SERVING
Calories: 345;
Fat: 30g;
Saturated Fat: 13g;
Sodium: 348mg;
Total Carbohydrates: 11g;
Net Carbohydrates: 6g;
Fiber: 5g;
Sugar: 2g;
Protein: 10g

1. Put the eggs, almond flour, milk, 4 tablespoons of melted butter, the coconut flour, vanilla, cinnamon, baking soda, and salt in a blender, and blend until smooth, scraping down the sides as needed.

2. Heat a large nonstick skillet or griddle over medium heat until hot, then brush with some of the remaining 2 tablespoons of melted butter.

3. Pour some of the pancake batter into the skillet to make pancakes the size you want. Cook for 2 minutes, or until the sides of each pancake begin to set and small bubbles appear in the center of each.

4. Flip the pancakes, and cook on the other side for about 2 minutes. Transfer to a serving plate.

5. Repeat with the remaining batter, using the remaining melted butter to grease the pan as needed.

Orange Ricotta–Stuffed Crêpes

GLUTEN-FREE, SOY-FREE, VEGETARIAN

Serves 4 (2 crêpes per person) | **PREP TIME:** 10 minutes | **COOK TIME:** 20 minutes

Filled with orange-infused cinnamon ricotta, these stuffed crêpes are a meal worthy of the weekend. I'm not normally a fan of nonstick cookware, but it's essential in this recipe to produce thin crêpes that don't stick to the pan.

4 ounces cream cheese, softened

4 large eggs

½ cup almond flour

2 tablespoons coconut flour

2 teaspoons pure vanilla extract, divided

6 drops liquid stevia, divided

1 cup whole-milk ricotta cheese

1 teaspoon ground cinnamon

Zest of 1 orange

6 teaspoons butter, divided

**PER SERVING
(2 CRÊPES)**
Calories: 384;
Fat: 30g;
Saturated Fat: 15g;
Sodium: 267mg;
Total Carbohydrates: 12g;
Net Carbohydrates: 8g;
Fiber: 4g;
Sugar: 1g;
Protein: 18g

1. To make the crêpe batter, put the cream cheese, eggs, almond flour, coconut flour, 1 teaspoon of vanilla, and 4 drops of liquid stevia in a blender, and blend until smooth, scraping down the sides as needed.

2. In a small bowl, combine the ricotta cheese, cinnamon, remaining 1 teaspoon vanilla, remaining 2 drops of liquid stevia, and the orange zest.

3. Heat a small nonstick skillet over medium heat until hot, then add 1 to 2 teaspoons of butter, and tilt to coat the bottom.

4. Pour in just enough of the crêpe batter to evenly coat the bottom of the skillet when tilted. Cook for about 45 seconds on the first side, or until just set.

5. Flip, and cook for 30 seconds. Carefully transfer to a plate, and repeat with the remaining 4 to 5 teaspoons of butter and the remaining crêpe batter.

6. To serve, place about 2 tablespoons of ricotta mixture atop each crêpe, and fold gently like an enchilada.

COOKING TIP: If you have the time and are feeling fancy, after filling each crêpe with the ricotta mixture, heat a tablespoon or two of butter in the skillet, and fry each crêpe on both sides for about 1 minute, or until browned.

Cauliflower Hash Browns

GLUTEN-FREE, NUT-FREE, SOY-FREE, VEGETARIAN

Serves 4 | **PREP TIME:** 15 minutes | **COOK TIME:** 8 to 10 minutes

Serve these crispy, crunchy hash browns with the Green Chile Scramble (page 10) for a hearty low-carb breakfast. The secret to getting the right texture with these hash browns is squeezing as much water as you can from the cauliflower.

1 small head cauliflower

1 teaspoon sea salt

1 large egg

¼ cup shredded
  Parmesan cheese

2 tablespoons coconut oil or
  extra-virgin olive oil

PER SERVING
Calories: 113;
Fat: 10g;
Saturated Fat: 7g;
Sodium: 568mg;
Total Carbohydrates: 4g;
Net Carbohydrates: 2g;
Fiber: 2g;
Sugar: 2g;
Protein: 5g

1. Grate the cauliflower in a food processor using the grater attachment or with the large holes of a box grater. You should have about 4 cups.

2. Transfer the cauliflower to a colander set over a large bowl, and season with the salt. Set aside for 10 minutes.

3. Squeeze the cauliflower in your hands to wring out as much moisture as possible, then transfer to a large bowl.

4. Add the egg and Parmesan cheese, and mix until just combined.

5. Heat a large nonstick skillet over medium-high heat, then pour in the coconut oil, and tilt to coat the bottom.

6. Meanwhile, form the cauliflower into small firm patties, and flatten each with your hand.

7. Once the oil is hot, working in batches if necessary, carefully place the patties in the skillet, and fry for 4 to 5 minutes on each side, or until deeply browned. Do not disturb while cooking. Transfer to a paper towel–lined plate.

COOKING TIP: Salt draws moisture out of the cauliflower before cooking. An alternative method is to microwave the grated cauliflower for 2 to 3 minutes, let it cool, then wring it out in a clean kitchen towel or several layers of cheesecloth.

Green Chile Scramble

GLUTEN-FREE, NUT-FREE, SOY-FREE, VEGETARIAN

Serves 4 | **PREP TIME:** 5 minutes | **COOK TIME:** 4 to 5 minutes

This tasty breakfast scramble has all of the flavors of chiles rellenos. But unlike the Mexican restaurant classic, this one is a cinch to make and has virtually no carbs. Purchase green chiles in the international foods section of the grocery store, using as many as you like according to how much spice you enjoy.

8 large eggs

2 tablespoons butter

¼ cup thinly sliced scallions, green and white parts

¼ cup crumbled Cotija cheese

2 to 4 tablespoons minced canned green chiles

2 tablespoons minced fresh cilantro

PER SERVING
Calories: 207;
Fat: 17g;
Saturated Fat: 8g;
Sodium: 307mg;
Total Carbohydrates: 2g;
Net Carbohydrates: 2g;
Fiber: 0g;
Sugar: 1g;
Protein: 13g

1. In a large bowl, whisk the eggs until they are thoroughly mixed.
2. Heat a large skillet over medium-high heat until hot, melt the butter, and tilt to coat the bottom.
3. Add the scallions, and sauté for about 2 minutes, or until fragrant and wilted.
4. Add the eggs, and use a spatula to stir them; they will cook quickly at this heat. Cook for about 2 minutes, or until nearly set.
5. Fold in the Cotija cheese and the green chiles, then remove the pan from the heat. Garnish with the cilantro.

INGREDIENT TIP: Cotija is a salty, hard Mexican cheese, so you may not need to add salt to the eggs. It doesn't melt the same way other cheeses do, but stays intact, making delicious pockets of cheesy flavor in this scramble. You can also use feta cheese.

Southwestern Veggie Egg Muffin Cups

GLUTEN-FREE, NUT-FREE, SOY-FREE, VEGETARIAN

Serves 6 | **PREP TIME:** 10 minutes | **COOK TIME:** 10 to 15 minutes

These egg muffin cups are perfect to prepare ahead of time, then freeze individually for quick on-the-go low-carb breakfasts. They're loaded with flavor from smoked paprika, fire-roasted vegetables, and spicy pepper jack cheese.

10 large eggs

1 teaspoon smoked paprika

1 teaspoon ground cumin

1 teaspoon sea salt

1 roasted red bell pepper, finely chopped

1 scallion, green and white parts, finely chopped

1 cup coarsely chopped frozen broccoli florets

½ cup frozen fire-roasted corn kernels

½ cup pepper jack cheese

1. Preheat the oven to 350°F.
2. Line the cups of a muffin tin with circles cut from parchment paper.
3. Put the eggs, paprika, cumin, and salt in a blender, and blend until smooth.
4. In a bowl, mix the bell pepper, scallion, broccoli, corn, and cheese, then divide among the muffin tin cups.
5. Pour the egg mixture into the muffin tin cups.
6. Carefully transfer the tin to the oven, and bake for 12 to 15 minutes, or until the eggs are just set. Let cool for a few minutes before serving.

PER SERVING
(2 EGG MUFFIN CUPS)
Calories: 164;
Fat: 10g;
Saturated Fat: 4g;
Sodium: 506mg;
Total Carbohydrates: 6g;
Net Carbohydrates: 5g;
Fiber: 1g;
Sugar: 2g;
Protein: 12g

COOKING TIP: Feel free to change up the fillings in this recipe. Broccoli, bacon, and cheddar are a classic combo. Or keep things vegetarian, and go with spinach, sundried tomato, fresh basil, and Parmesan cheese for some hearty Italian flavors.

Farmers' Market Breakfast Hash

DAIRY-FREE, GLUTEN-FREE, NUT-FREE, SOY-FREE, VEGETARIAN

Serves 4 | **PREP TIME:** 10 minutes | **COOK TIME:** 15 to 20 minutes

This breakfast hash is loaded with healthy fiber and phytonutrients. Fiber is in short supply in the typical American diet—97 percent of us don't meet the minimum daily recommendation of 25 grams—and it can be easy to overlook on a low-carb diet. That's a mistake! Fiber is essential in helping our bodies rid themselves of toxins, lower our cholesterol, and improve our gut health. Here's a delicious way to boost your fiber intake and keep your carbs in check.

1 head broccoli, cut into small florets

1 red bell pepper, cut into strips

1 green bell pepper, cut into strips

1 onion, halved and thinly sliced

¼ cup coarsely chopped fresh herbs, such as parsley, basil, thyme, and rosemary

3 tablespoons extra-virgin olive oil or coconut oil, divided

Sea salt

Freshly ground black pepper

8 large eggs

PER SERVING
Calories: 269;
Fat: 20g;
Saturated Fat: 4g;
Sodium: 209mg;
Total Carbohydrates: 12g;
Net Carbohydrates: 8g;
Fiber: 4g;
Sugar: 4g;
Protein: 14g

1. Preheat the oven to 425°F. Line a rimmed baking sheet with parchment paper.

2. Spread the broccoli, bell peppers, onion, and herbs onto the baking sheet, then drizzle with 2 tablespoons of oil, and toss gently to coat. Season with salt and pepper.

3. Transfer the baking sheet to the oven, and roast for 15 to 20 minutes, or until the vegetables are gently browned and tender.

4. Meanwhile, heat a large skillet over medium-high heat until hot, then pour in the remaining 1 tablespoon of oil, and tilt to coat the bottom.

5. Add the eggs, and fry until they reach your desired level of doneness.

6. To serve, divide the roasted vegetables among 4 serving plates, and top with the fried eggs.

COOKING TIP: A convection oven will speed the cooking time of any dish. It is particularly helpful for roasting vegetables because the circulating air draws moisture away from them, increasing browning.

Spanakopita Frittata

GLUTEN-FREE, NUT-FREE, SOY-FREE, VEGETARIAN

Serves 6 | **PREP TIME:** 5 minutes | **COOK TIME:** 25 minutes

Spanakopita is a Greek puff pastry stuffed with spinach and feta cheese. In this low-carb recipe makeover, you get all of the familiar flavors without all of the carbs. Use a good-quality sheep's milk feta for the most authentic flavor.

2 tablespoons extra-virgin
olive oil

1 small onion, finely chopped

2 garlic cloves, minced

2 cups packed coarsely
chopped fresh spinach

2 teaspoons dried dill

1 cup minced fresh
flat-leaf parsley

10 ounces feta cheese,
crumbled

8 large eggs, whisked

PER SERVING
Calories: 262;
Fat: 21g;
Saturated Fat: 10g;
Sodium: 624mg;
Total Carbohydrates: 5g;
Net Carbohydrates: 4g;
Fiber: 1g;
Sugar: 3g;
Protein: 15g

1. Preheat the oven to 400°F.
2. Heat a large cast-iron skillet or other ovenproof skillet over medium heat until hot, then pour in the oil, and tilt to coat the bottom.
3. Add the onion and garlic, and cook for 2 to 3 minutes, or until fragrant and somewhat softened.
4. Add the spinach, and cook for 2 to 3 minutes, or until it releases its liquid.
5. Stir in the dill and parsley.
6. Sprinkle the feta cheese on top, then pour in the eggs.
7. Transfer the skillet to the oven, and bake for 20 minutes, or until the eggs are set.

INGREDIENT TIP: If you prefer to use frozen spinach, use 1 cup and defrost under running water. With your hands, wring out as much moisture as you can before adding the spinach to the pan.

Pizza Frittata

GLUTEN-FREE, SOY-FREE

Serves 4 | **PREP TIME:** 5 minutes | **COOK TIME:** 25 minutes

Pizza for breakfast? No, this isn't the flavorless, post-party college standby you may have suffered through in the past. It is fresh, hot, and absolutely delicious! Spicy Italian sausage, fragrant sundried tomatoes, and fresh basil meld into a creamy melty mix of eggs and Parmesan.

2 links hot Italian sausage, casings removed

8 large eggs

½ cup half-and-half

½ cup almond flour

½ teaspoon sea salt

¼ cup sundried tomatoes, cut into thin strips

¼ cup grated Parmesan cheese

¼ cup coarsely chopped fresh basil

PER SERVING
Calories: 261;
Fat: 19g;
Saturated Fat: 7g;
Sodium: 349mg;
Total Carbohydrates: 6g;
Net Carbohydrates: 5g;
Fiber: 1g;
Sugar: 2g;
Protein: 18g

1. Preheat the oven to 400°F.
2. Heat a large cast-iron skillet or other ovenproof skillet over medium-high heat until hot.
3. Toss in the sausage, and cook for 5 minutes, or until barely cooked through.
4. Put the eggs, half-and-half, almond flour, and salt in a blender, and blend until mixed, scraping down the sides as needed.
5. Scatter the sundried tomatoes, Parmesan cheese, and basil over the cooked sausage in the skillet, then pour the egg mixture over it.
6. Transfer the skillet to the oven, and bake for 20 minutes, or until the eggs are set.

VARIATION TIP: For a milder flavor, choose pancetta or diced bacon instead of Italian sausage.

Avocado-Citrus Salad, page 24

2

snacks, salads, and sides

Parmesan Crisps

GLUTEN-FREE, NUT-FREE, SOY-FREE, VEGETARIAN

Serves 4 (16 crisps total) | **PREP TIME:** 5 minutes | **COOK TIME:** 5 minutes

Sometimes you just miss the satisfying crunch of a chip. These Parmesan crisps deliver—literally! You can load them with all kinds of savory dips, from Olive Tapenade (page 19) to Mediterranean Zucchini Hummus (page 20). And, with only one ingredient, they're almost too easy.

1 cup grated Parmesan cheese

**PER SERVING
(4 CRISPS)**
Calories: 90;
Fat: 6g;
Saturated Fat: 4g;
Sodium: 260mg;
Total Carbohydrates: 1g;
Net Carbohydrates: 1g;
Fiber: 0g;
Sugar: 0g;
Protein: 9g

1. Preheat the oven to 400°F. Line a rimmed baking sheet with parchment paper, or use a silicone baking mat.

2. Place 1 tablespoon of the Parmesan cheese on the baking sheet, spreading it slightly to form a circle.

3. Repeat with the remaining cheese, leaving a few inches between each spoonful of cheese (you should end up with about 16 total).

4. Transfer the baking sheet to the oven, and bake for 5 minutes, or until the cheese is melted and beginning to bubble. Let cool thoroughly before lifting from the pan.

VARIATION TIP: Spice things up with ¼ teaspoon of cayenne pepper mixed into the cheese, or go in an herbal direction with 1 teaspoon of dried Italian herb blend.

Olive Tapenade

DAIRY-FREE, GLUTEN-FREE, NUT-FREE, SOY-FREE, VEGAN

Makes 1 cup (4 servings) | **PREP TIME:** 5 minutes

In college I worked in a Tuscan restaurant where we served a similar olive tapenade to guests when they arrived. It is delicious with Parmesan Crisps (page 18) or as a topping for fish.

1 garlic clove, minced

1 cup assorted gourmet
    olives, pitted

2 tablespoons minced sundried
    tomatoes

2 tablespoons minced fresh
    flat-leaf parsley

1 tablespoon capers, drained

1 tablespoon minced fresh basil

1 teaspoon minced
    fresh oregano

¼ cup extra-virgin olive oil

**PER SERVING
(¼ CUP)**
Calories: 191;
Fat: 20g;
Saturated Fat: 2g;
Sodium: 445mg;
Total Carbohydrates: 5g;
Net Carbohydrates: 4g;
Fiber: 1g;
Sugar: 1g;
Protein: 1g

1. Put the garlic, olives, sundried tomatoes, parsley, capers, basil, and oregano in a small food processor, and pulse until the mixture is finely ground and nearly a paste.

2. Slowly drizzle in the oil, and pulse until it is all incorporated.

3. Store in a covered container in the refrigerator for up to 1 week.

INGREDIENT TIP: Use the best olives and olive oil you can find. I prefer the olives at the fresh bar at specialty markets. Jarred varieties work well, too. Just don't use the canned olives that you might put on a pizza.

Mediterranean Zucchini Hummus

DAIRY-FREE, GLUTEN-FREE, SOY-FREE, VEGAN

Makes 1 cup (4 servings) | **PREP TIME:** 5 minutes

This hummus has a fraction of the carbs of traditional chickpea-based hummus, but it still has all the scrumptious flavors of garlic, lemon, tahini, and olive oil. Top it with toasted pine nuts, sundried tomatoes, and herbs for an elegant presentation. Serve with sliced vegetables or Parmesan Crisps (page 18) for a hearty appetizer or a simple low-carb snack.

2 small zucchini, peeled
  and seeded

2 garlic cloves, minced

2 tablespoons tahini

1 teaspoon freshly squeezed
  lemon juice

¼ cup extra-virgin olive oil,
  plus more for drizzling

Sea salt

2 tablespoons toasted
  pine nuts

2 tablespoons finely chopped
  sundried tomatoes

1 tablespoon fresh minced
  flat-leaf parsley

1. Put the zucchini, garlic, tahini, and lemon juice in a small food processor, and blend until mostly smooth.

2. Slowly drizzle in the oil, and pulse until it is all incorporated. Season with salt.

3. Transfer the hummus to a serving bowl, and top with the pine nuts, sundried tomatoes, and parsley. Drizzle with additional oil. Store in a covered container in the refrigerator for up to 4 days.

**PER SERVING
(¼ CUP)**
Calories: 198;
Fat: 20g;
Saturated Fat: 3g;
Sodium: 63mg;
Total Carbohydrates: 6g;
Net Carbohydrates: 4g;
Fiber: 2g;
Sugar: 2g;
Protein: 3g

Tzatziki Dip with Vegetables

GLUTEN-FREE, NUT-FREE, SOY-FREE, VEGETARIAN

Serves 8 | **PREP TIME:** 10 minutes

Greek yogurt lends itself well to this classic Middle Eastern dip because it is traditionally made with strained yogurt. It's naturally low in carbs and pairs well with fresh vegetables, as in the recipe, or alongside the Roasted Eggplant with Ground Lamb and Pine Nuts (page 73).

2 cups whole-milk
   Greek yogurt

1 small cucumber, peeled and
   finely diced

3 garlic cloves, minced

2 tablespoons minced fresh dill

2 tablespoons minced
   fresh mint

1 tablespoon extra-virgin
   olive oil

2 teaspoons freshly squeezed
   lemon juice

½ teaspoon sea salt

Freshly ground black pepper

2 pounds assorted nonstarchy
   vegetables, such as green
   beans, cucumbers, red bell
   peppers, and carrots, cut
   into sticks, for dipping

1. In a medium bowl, combine the yogurt, cucumber, garlic, dill, mint, oil, lemon juice, salt, and pepper, whisking to mix well. Season with additional salt and black pepper.

2. Serve in a small bowl as a dip alongside the veggies.

COOKING TIP: If there is enough room in your Greek yogurt container, you can mix everything right in there! Just top with the lid and shake vigorously. This makes cleanup even easier.

PER SERVING
Calories: 114;
Fat: 4g;
Saturated Fat: 2g;
Sodium: 180mg;
Total Carbohydrates: 13g;
Net Carbohydrates: 9g;
Fiber: 4g;
Sugar: 6g;
Protein: 7g

Cucumber Smoked Salmon Bites

GLUTEN-FREE, NUT-FREE, SOY-FREE

Serves 4 | **PREP TIME:** 5 minutes

My best friend, Marcella, served these gorgeous appetizers for my bridal shower, and they were the runaway hit of the party. The original recipe was served on artisan kettle-roasted potato chips. This lighter version is a little more wedding dress–friendly and still has all the tasty flavor of the original.

1 medium to large cucumber, peeled and cut into ¼-inch-thick slices

8 ounces goat cheese, cut into ¼-inch-thick slices

4 ounces cold-smoked salmon or lox

2 tablespoons coarsely chopped fresh dill

Freshly ground black pepper

1. Top each cucumber slice with a slice of goat cheese and a piece of salmon.
2. Arrange the appetizers on a serving platter, and garnish with the dill and black pepper.

SUBSTITUTION TIP: If you're not a fan of the tangy flavor of goat cheese, cream cheese will work just fine here.

PER SERVING
Calories: 301;
Fat: 22g;
Saturated Fat: 14g;
Sodium: 565mg;
Total Carbohydrates: 4g;
Net Carbohydrates: 3g;
Fiber: 1g;
Sugar: 3g;
Protein: 23g

Creamy Avocado Gazpacho

DAIRY-FREE, GLUTEN-FREE, NUT-FREE, SOY-FREE, VEGAN

Serves 4 | **PREP TIME:** 10 minutes

This raw vegan soup makes a delicious starter during the hot summer months. The vibrant green color belies its almost magical secret—it's brimming with healthy plant nutrients. The celery brings antioxidants and enzymes, which help reduce oxidative stress and improve digestion.

1 celery stalk, chopped

1 medium cucumber, peeled, seeded, and diced

1 large avocado, pitted, peeled, and diced

1 large handful coarsely chopped fresh cilantro

1 large handful coarsely chopped fresh flat-leaf parsley

1 shallot, peeled and coarsely chopped

1 lime, peeled

2 cups water

½ teaspoon sea salt

1. Put the celery, cucumber, avocado, cilantro, parsley, shallot, lime, water, and salt in a blender, and purée until smooth, scraping down the sides as needed.
2. Divide among 4 serving bowls, and serve chilled.

COOKING TIP: For more texture, reserve half of the diced cucumber and avocado, and stir it into the puréed soup. Reduce the water by ½ cup.

PER SERVING
Calories: 96;
Fat: 7g;
Saturated Fat: 1g;
Sodium: 253mg;
Total Carbohydrates: 10g;
Net Carbohydrates: 6g;
Fiber: 4g;
Sugar: 2g;
Protein: 2g

Avocado-Citrus Salad

DAIRY-FREE, GLUTEN-FREE, NUT-FREE, SOY-FREE, VEGAN

Serves 4 | **PREP TIME:** 10 minutes

Avocado and citrus are a natural combination. The acid of the grapefruit cuts through the richness of the avocado. A little flaky sea salt blunts any bitterness, and a fruity, spicy olive oil really completes the flavor. Or you can sprinkle on my favorite spice to add to foods at the table—the Japanese condiment togarashi. It's a blend of orange peel, sesame seeds, chile, and seaweed. It may sound unusual, but it has just the right blend of flavors to make people say, "What is in this?"

1 head butter lettuce, leaves torn into bite-size pieces

2 large avocados, pitted and cut into wedges

2 large grapefruits, peeled and *suprêmed* (see Cooking Tip)

2 tablespoons extra-virgin olive oil

Pinch red pepper flakes

Sea salt

1. Spread the lettuce on a serving platter.
2. Top with the avocado and grapefruit segments.
3. Squeeze the grapefruit membranes (see the tip below) over the salad.
4. Drizzle with the oil, and season with red pepper flakes and sea salt.

COOKING TIP: To *suprême* citrus fruits, such as grapefruits and oranges, simply means to cut into segments and remove the membranes, pith, and seeds. To do this, cut off each end of the fruit, stand it on one end, and slice away the peel and all of the pith. Using a paring knife, slice between each of the membranes.

PER SERVING
Calories: 269;
Fat: 21g;
Saturated Fat: 3g;
Sodium: 70mg;
Total Carbohydrates: 23g;
Net Carbohydrates: 14g;
Fiber: 9g;
Sugar: 13g;
Protein: 3g

Caprese Salad

GLUTEN-FREE, NUT-FREE, SOY-FREE, VEGETARIAN

Serves 4 | **PREP TIME:** 10 minutes

Reserve this classic Italian salad for late summer, when tomatoes are at their peak. It makes a delicious appetizer or a light meal when you don't want to heat up the oven or stove. It's ready in minutes. Use the best balsamic vinegar you can find for the dressing—you will taste a difference.

2 (4-ounce) balls fresh mozzarella cheese, cut into ½-inch pieces

2 medium to large vine-ripe tomatoes, cut into ½-inch pieces

2 tablespoons balsamic vinegar

2 tablespoons extra-virgin olive oil

4 fresh basil leaves, minced

Sea salt

Freshly ground black pepper

PER SERVING
Calories: 233;
Fat: 21g;
Saturated Fat: 9g;
Sodium: 45mg;
Total Carbohydrates: 3g;
Net Carbohydrates: 2g;
Fiber: 1g;
Sugar: 2g;
Protein: 11g

1. Layer the mozzarella and tomatoes on individual serving plates.
2. Drizzle with the vinegar and oil, and top with the fresh basil. Season with salt and pepper.

INGREDIENT TIP: Find fresh mozzarella in the refrigerated deli section. It will be soaking in brine or water in a plastic container.

Wilted Spinach Salad with Mushrooms and Bacon

DAIRY-FREE, GLUTEN-FREE, NUT-FREE, SOY-FREE

Serves 4 | **PREP TIME:** 5 minutes | **COOK TIME:** 20 minutes

This recipe falls somewhere between a salad and a side dish. Although you begin with mounds of fresh spinach, it cooks down to much more manageable portions. To make it a complete meal, top each portion with a poached egg or two.

4 slices applewood-smoked
   bacon, thinly sliced
8 ounces cremini mushrooms,
   cut into ¼-inch-thick slices
1 garlic clove, minced
1 pound fresh spinach
1 teaspoon apple cider vinegar
Sea salt

PER SERVING
Calories: 146;
Fat: 8g;
Saturated Fat: 3g;
Sodium: 591mg;
Total Carbohydrates: 7g;
Net Carbohydrates: 4g;
Fiber: 3g;
Sugar: 2g;
Protein: 12g

1. Heat a large skillet over medium heat until hot.
2. Place the bacon in the skillet in a single layer, and cook until crisp-tender, about 10 minutes. Use a slotted spoon to transfer to a separate plate.
3. Working in 2 batches, add the mushrooms to the skillet in a single layer, and sear for about 2 minutes on each side, or until gently browned. Use a slotted spoon to transfer to a separate plate.
4. Add the garlic to the skillet, and cook for a few seconds, or just until fragrant.
5. Add the spinach, and use tongs to toss for about 2 minutes, or until it is just wilted but before the spinach has released much water.
6. Add the apple cider vinegar, bacon, and mushrooms and toss gently to mix. Remove from the heat, and serve warm.

INGREDIENT TIP: Choose uncured bacon (bacon that hasn't been cured with sodium nitrite) from sustainably raised and harvested pork for the best flavor.

Celery Root Purée

GLUTEN-FREE, NUT-FREE, SOY-FREE, VEGETARIAN

Serves 4 | **PREP TIME:** 5 minutes | **COOK TIME:** 25 minutes

This flavorful purée is the perfect stand-in for mashed potatoes. Don't be intimidated by celery root's less-than-gorgeous exterior. Cut it away with a chef's knife to reveal its creamy white center. Blended in half-and-half, it becomes soft and creamy.

2 celery roots, peeled and diced

1 small white onion, diced

½ cup half-and-half

2 tablespoons butter

1 teaspoon sea salt

PER SERVING
Calories: 163;
Fat: 10g;
Saturated Fat: 6g;
Sodium: 678mg;
Total Carbohydrates: 16g;
Net Carbohydrates. 12g;
Fiber: 4g;
Sugar: 3g;
Protein: 4g

1. Place the celery roots and onion in a steamer basket set in a large pot with about 1 inch of water.

2. Bring the water to a gentle simmer over medium heat, cover, and cook for 20 to 25 minutes, or until the celery roots are tender.

3. Transfer the celery roots and onion to a blender.

4. Add the half-and-half, butter, and salt, and blend until smooth, adding enough of the cooking liquid to achieve the desired consistency and scraping down the sides as needed.

COOKING TIP: To peel the celery root, cut off both ends and stand it on one end on a cutting board. Use a chef's knife to cut off the peel all the way around. Brush any dirt from the cutting board before dicing the root.

Baked Spaghetti Squash

DAIRY-FREE, GLUTEN-FREE, NUT-FREE, SOY-FREE, VEGAN

Serves 4 | **PREP TIME:** 5 minutes | **COOK TIME:** 25 minutes

I had no idea just how versatile spaghetti squash was until I finally gave it a try. Who knew—it's a lot like spaghetti! The trick to getting long, pretty noodles is slicing the squash into rings crosswise, and not slicing it in half lengthwise, as is often recommended. It's a little more work, but it creates the texture you want in something that's supposed to replace pasta. Serve spaghetti squash with marinara sauce or pesto to create a tasty side dish. It's also delicious in the Soy-Ginger Chicken and Squash Noodle Bowls (page 46).

1 large spaghetti squash
   (about 2 pounds)

Sea salt

PER SERVING
Calories: 70;
Fat: 1g;
Saturated Fat: 0g;
Sodium: 97mg;
Total Carbohydrates: 16g;
Net Carbohydrates: 16g;
Fiber: 0g;
Sugar: 0g;
Protein: 2g

1. Preheat the oven to 350°F. Line a rimmed baking sheet with parchment paper.
2. Cut the spaghetti squash crosswise into 1-inch-thick rings, and scrape away the seeds and strings from the centers.
3. Place the squash rings on the baking sheet in a single layer.
4. Transfer the baking sheet to the oven, and bake for 25 minutes, or until the squash is tender but not yet browned.
5. Carefully use a fork to scrape the insides of the squash into a serving bowl, and discard the outer skins. Season with salt.

Cauli Rice

DAIRY-FREE, GLUTEN-FREE, NUT-FREE, SOY-FREE, VEGAN

Serves 4 | **PREP TIME:** 15 minutes | **COOK TIME:** 5 minutes

Cauliflower rice might just be the difference between success and failure on a low-carb diet. If you're used to eating filling meals with more volume, the switch to a low-carb diet can be a little disappointing. Calorie for calorie, fat and protein take up less space on the plate than carbohydrates do. Cauli rice to the rescue! It's a tasty stand-in for traditional rice and has less than 100 calories and only 4 grams of net carbs per generous serving.

1 medium head cauliflower, cored and cut into florets

Sea salt

1 tablespoon canola oil

PER SERVING
Calories: 67;
Fat: 4g;
Saturated Fat: 0g;
Sodium: 102mg;
Total Carbohydrates: 8g;
Net Carbohydrates: 4g;
Fiber: 4g;
Sugar: 4g;
Protein: 3g

1. Put the cauliflower in a food processor fitted with the standard blade, and pulse until it resembles small grains of rice. (Or grate it on a box grater using the largest holes.)

2. Place the cauliflower into a colander set over a bowl, and season generously with salt. Let rest for 10 minutes to draw out some of the moisture.

3. Rinse the cauliflower with water, then wring out some of the moisture with your hands.

4. Heat a large skillet over medium-high heat until hot, then add the oil, and tilt to coat the bottom.

5. Add the cauliflower, and sauté for about 5 minutes, or until just tender but not soft.

COOKING TIP: Another way to wring the moisture out of the grated cauliflower is to place it in a clean kitchen towel, then twist the towel until the cauliflower releases its moisture.

Oven-Roasted Brussels Sprouts

DAIRY-FREE, GLUTEN-FREE, NUT-FREE, SOY-FREE, VEGAN

Serves 4 | **PREP TIME:** 10 minutes | **COOK TIME:** 15 to 20 minutes

This recipe will convert even the most ardent Brussels sprouts skeptic. The trick is getting a nice caramelization on the vegetables, which is achieved through roasting at high (but not too high) heat. This nicely browns the cut side of the sprouts while cooking them all the way through without overcooking.

1 pound Brussels sprouts,
   trimmed and halved

3 tablespoons extra-virgin
   olive oil

Sea salt

Freshly ground black pepper

1½ tablespoons
   balsamic vinegar

PER SERVING
Calories: 140;
Fat: 11g;
Saturated Fat: 2g;
Sodium: 40mg;
Total Carbohydrates: 10g;
Net Carbohydrates: 6g;
Fiber: 4g;
Sugar: 3g;
Protein: 4g

1. Preheat the oven to 375°F.
2. Toss the Brussels sprouts with the oil, then spread them out in a single layer, cut sides down, on a rimmed baking sheet. Season with salt and pepper.
3. Transfer the baking sheet to the oven, and bake for 15 minutes.
4. Drizzle the sprouts with the balsamic vinegar, tossing to coat.
5. Return the baking sheet to the oven, and bake for another 3 to 5 minutes, or until the vinegar has caramelized but not burned. Serve immediately.

COOKING TIP: To clean and trim the Brussels sprouts, place them in a large bowl of water. Use a paring knife to slice off the bottom and any tough outer leaves, then slice in half.

Green Beans with Lemon and Mint

DAIRY-FREE, GLUTEN-FREE, NUT-FREE, SOY-FREE, VEGAN

Serves 4 | **PREP TIME:** 5 minutes | **COOK TIME:** 5 to 10 minutes

Steamed green beans get an instant upgrade with tangy lemon juice, cooling mint leaves, and a splash of olive oil. Just a couple of ingredients make all the difference. Make it even easier by blanching a batch of green beans on the weekend, so you have cooked beans ready in the refrigerator during the weekdays. You can also serve this dish chilled.

1 pound green beans, trimmed

1 tablespoon extra-virgin olive oil

Zest and juice of 1 lemon

2 tablespoons minced fresh mint

Sea salt

PER SERVING
Calories: 66;
Fat: 4g;
Saturated Fat: 1g;
Sodium: 66mg;
Total Carbohydrates: 8g;
Net Carbohydrates: 4g;
Fiber: 4g;
Sugar: 2g;
Protein: 2g

1. Place the green beans in a steamer basket set in a large pot with about 1 inch of water.
2. Bring the water to a gentle simmer over medium heat, cover, and cook for 7 to 8 minutes, or until the green beans are tender.
3. Transfer the beans to a serving bowl, and top with the oil, lemon zest and juice, and mint. Season with salt and serve warm.

VARIATION TIP: Preserved lemons add another layer of complexity to this dish. If you want to try them, you can usually find them in the international or gourmet foods section of your grocery store. A little goes a long way, so try adding about ¼ of a preserved lemon, flesh discarded and peel finely diced, to start.

Curry Roasted Cauliflower

DAIRY-FREE, GLUTEN-FREE, NUT-FREE, SOY-FREE, VEGAN

Serves 4 | **PREP TIME:** 5 minutes | **COOK TIME:** 20 to 25 minutes

Cauliflower gets so many makeovers in low-carb cooking, but sometimes it's nice just to let it be itself. The tender cruciferous vegetable becomes crisp-tender when roasted and soaks up all the delicious flavor of curry powder in this healthy side dish.

1 head cauliflower, cored and
cut into florets

2 tablespoons coconut
oil, melted

1 tablespoon curry powder

½ teaspoon sea salt

PER SERVING
Calories: 100;
Fat: 7g;
Saturated Fat: 6g;
Sodium: 278mg;
Total Carbohydrates: 9g;
Net Carbohydrates: 5g;
Fiber: 4g;
Sugar: 4g;
Protein: 3g

1. Preheat the oven to 375°F.
2. Put the cauliflower in a large bowl, and drizzle with the oil. Use your hands to toss until well coated.
3. Add the curry powder and salt, and toss thoroughly to coat.
4. Spread the cauliflower onto a rimmed baking sheet in a single layer, and bake for 20 to 25 minutes, or until the cauliflower is crisp-tender and well browned.

COOKING TIP: You could toss the cauliflower with the oil and curry powder directly on the baking sheet, but this will cause some of the curry powder to stick to the pan and burn.

Broccolini with Dijon Balsamic Mayo and Roasted Red Peppers

DAIRY-FREE, GLUTEN-FREE, NUT-FREE, SOY-FREE, VEGETARIAN

Serves 4 | **PREP TIME:** 5 minutes | **COOK TIME:** 2 to 3 minutes

Broccolini is similar to broccoli but with smaller florets and longer stalks. It is a hybrid of broccoli and gai lan (Chinese broccoli). This addictive appetizer is adapted from one of my favorite vegan cookbooks, **Vedge,** *from the Philadelphia restaurant by the same name. The recipe is naturally low in carbs but really packs a flavor punch.*

1 small garlic clove, minced

¼ cup mayonnaise

1 teaspoon balsamic vinegar

½ teaspoon Dijon mustard

Sea salt

2 bunches broccolini

1 tablespoon extra-virgin olive oil

2 roasted red peppers, thinly sliced

1. To make the dressing, in a small bowl, whisk the garlic, mayonnaise, vinegar, and mustard to combine. Season with salt.
2. Bring a large pot of salted water to a boil over high heat.
3. Plunge the broccolini into the water, and cook for 2 to 3 minutes, or until bright green and barely tender.
4. Drain the broccolini. In a large bowl, toss with the oil.
5. To serve, spread a spoonful of the dressing onto each plate, top with the broccolini, then the roasted peppers.

SUBSTITUTION TIP: To make this vegan, use a vegan mayonnaise. This will not change the nutrition information substantially.

PER SERVING
Calories: 136;
Fat: 9g;
Saturated Fat: 1g;
Sodium: 320mg;
Total Carbohydrates: 10g;
Net Carbohydrates: 7g;
Fiber: 3g;
Sugar: 4g;
Protein: 4g

Creamed Broccoli

GLUTEN-FREE, NUT-FREE, SOY-FREE

Serves 4 | **PREP TIME:** 5 minutes | **COOK TIME:** 20 minutes

Charring the broccoli first before steaming it deepens the flavor of this healthy side dish. To achieve a proper char, avoid stirring the broccoli as it sears in step 2. This will contribute to browning, which brings complexity to any dish. Just don't let it sit too long—you're not looking for blackened broccoli here.

2 tablespoons extra-virgin
   olive oil
2 heads broccoli (about
   2 pounds total), cut
   into florets
1 large garlic clove, smashed
Pinch red pepper flakes
½ cup chicken broth
½ cup whole-milk plain yogurt
Sea salt

PER SERVING
Calories: 162;
Fat: 9g;
Saturated Fat: 2g;
Sodium: 243mg;
Total Carbohydrates: 17g;
Net Carbohydrates: 10g;
Fiber: 7g;
Sugar: 5g;
Protein: 8g

1. Heat a large skillet over medium-high heat, then pour in the oil, and tilt to coat the bottom.

2. Working in 2 batches, add the broccoli in a single layer to the skillet, and cook undisturbed for about 2 minutes, or until gently browned. Transfer to a large dish. Repeat with the remaining broccoli.

3. Return all the broccoli to the skillet, then add the garlic and red pepper flakes, and cook for a few seconds, or until the garlic is fragrant.

4. Add the broth, and cover the pan with a tight-fitting lid.

5. Reduce the heat to medium-low, and cook for about 10 minutes, or until the broccoli is tender.

6. Remove the lid. Use an immersion blender or potato masher to mash the broccoli until it is somewhat smooth but large chunks still remain.

7. Stir in the yogurt and season with salt.

SUBSTITUTION TIP: To make this dish vegan, use vegetable broth and a vegan yogurt, such as plain cashew yogurt.

Pancetta and Tomato Roasted Chicken with Mozzarella, page 49

3

chicken

Pan-Seared Chicken with Zucchini

DAIRY-FREE, GLUTEN-FREE, NUT-FREE, SOY-FREE

Serves 2 | **PREP TIME:** 5 minutes | **COOK TIME:** 15 minutes

This is hands down my favorite chicken dinner to make when I really don't have much energy, but I want a meal that tastes like it came straight from a restaurant. The wine reduction may sound fancy, but it's a really simple technique to get the last bits of goodness out of any pan in which you've seared meat.

1 tablespoon extra-virgin
   olive oil
4 boneless, skinless
   chicken thighs
Sea salt
Freshly ground black pepper
2 medium zucchini, cut into
   ½-inch pieces
1 teaspoon fresh thyme
¼ cup dry red wine

PER SERVING
Calories: 377;
Fat: 16g;
Saturated Fat: 3g;
Sodium: 338mg;
Total Carbohydrates: 8g;
Net Carbohydrates: 6g;
Fiber: 2g;
Sugar: 4g;
Protein: 47g

1. Heat a large skillet over medium-high heat until hot, then pour in the oil, and tilt to coat the bottom.
2. Pat the chicken dry with paper towels, and season generously with salt and pepper.
3. Add the chicken to the skillet, and sear for 4 to 5 minutes.
4. Flip, and sear for 4 minutes. Transfer the chicken to a cutting board to rest.
5. Add the zucchini and thyme to the skillet, and sear for 2 to 3 minutes, or until nicely browned but not too soft.
6. Divide the zucchini between 2 serving plates, and top with the chicken.
7. Carefully add the red wine to the skillet, and simmer for about 2 minutes, or until reduced by half, using a wooden spoon to scrape up any browned bits from the bottom of the pan. Pour the wine reduction over the chicken and zucchini.

VARIATION TIP: If you prefer to use chicken breasts, use 2 medium breasts. Place them between 2 sheets of parchment paper and pound gently with the flat side of a meat cleaver until they're about ½-inch thick all the way through. Cook as indicated above.

Pesto Chicken with Zucchini Noodles

GLUTEN-FREE, SOY-FREE

Serves 4 | **PREP TIME:** 10 minutes | **COOK TIME:** 10 minutes

I recently learned a new method for making pesto that's renewed my love for this classic sauce—making it in a mortar and pestle. The coarse pine nuts and sea salt help extract the flavors from the basil as you mash them. If you have one, great. If not, just use a food processor. I use cooked chicken in this recipe to save time, but you can also cook about 1 pound of boneless, skinless chicken thighs in the pan until cooked through before adding the zucchini noodles.

¼ cup pine nuts

1 garlic clove

¼ teaspoon coarse sea salt

2 cups packed basil leaves

¼ cup plus 1 tablespoon
   extra-virgin olive oil, divided

¼ cup grated Parmesan cheese,
   plus more for serving

2 medium zucchini, spiralized

2 cups shredded cooked
   chicken, light and dark meat

PER SERVING
Calories: 353;
Fat: 27g;
Saturated Fat: 5g;
Sodium: 239mg;
Total Carbohydrates: 5g;
Net Carbohydrates: 3g;
Fiber: 2g;
Sugar: 2g;
Protein: 25g

1. To make the pesto, put the pine nuts in a dry pan, and lightly toast over medium heat, stirring, for about 3 minutes, or until they are fragrant.

2. Transfer to a mortar and pestle, and grind coarsely.

3. Add the garlic and salt, and pound until you have a thick paste.

4. Add the basil, and work into the pine nuts until completely incorporated, adding ¼ cup of oil as you go.

5. Stir in the Parmesan cheese.

6. Heat a large skillet over medium-high heat until hot, then pour in the remaining 1 tablespoon of oil, and tilt to coat the bottom.

7. Add the zucchini, and cook for about 1 minute, stirring frequently.

8. Add the chicken, and cook for about 2 minutes, or until heated through.

9. Remove from the heat, and add the pesto, tossing gently to coat the noodles and chicken. Serve with additional Parmesan.

COOKING TIP: If you don't have a spiralizer, cut the zucchini into long, thin "fettuccine" noodles. Use a vegetable peeler to get the flat slices, then stack them up, and cut with a knife to form thin noodles.

Yogurt and Tahini Chicken with Tomato-Cucumber Salad

GLUTEN-FREE, SOY-FREE

Serves 4 | **PREP TIME:** 10 minutes | **COOK TIME:** 10 to 15 minutes

Inspired by tandoori chicken but with a Middle Eastern twist, this crispy baked chicken is packed with flavor and protein. Almond flour replaces traditional bread crumbs to keep things low-carb. A refreshing tomato-cucumber salad balances out the rich, bold flavors of the chicken.

¼ cup whole-milk plain yogurt

¼ cup tahini

Zest and juice of 2 lemons

1 teaspoon minced garlic

1 teaspoon sea salt

½ cup almond flour

¼ teaspoon cayenne pepper

1 pound chicken breast tenders

1 pint grape tomatoes, halved

1 cucumber, peeled and diced

½ cup chopped fresh
    flat-leaf parsley

1 tablespoon red-wine vinegar

Sea salt

Freshly ground black pepper

PER SERVING
Calories: 298;
Fat: 14g;
Saturated Fat: 2g;
Sodium: 155mg;
Total Carbohydrates: 13g;
Net Carbohydrates: 9g;
Fiber: 4g;
Sugar: 5g;
Protein: 33g

1. Preheat the oven to 400°F. Line a rimmed baking sheet with parchment paper.

2. In a shallow dish, whisk the yogurt, tahini, lemon zest and juice, garlic, and salt.

3. In another dish, combine the almond flour and cayenne pepper.

4. Dredge each of the chicken pieces in the yogurt mixture, then dredge in the almond flour.

5. Place the chicken on the baking sheet in a single layer, then transfer to the oven, and bake for 12 to 15 minutes, or until cooked through.

6. Meanwhile, in a bowl, combine the tomatoes, cucumber, parsley, and red-wine vinegar. Season with salt and pepper.

7. Serve the chicken with the salad on the side.

Chicken Provençal

DAIRY-FREE, GLUTEN-FREE, NUT-FREE, SOY-FREE

Serves 4 | **PREP TIME:** 10 minutes | **COOK TIME:** 20 minutes

This one-pan low-carb supper gets better as it sits, so it's perfect for those lazy days when you want to prepare dinner a couple hours ahead of time. Use the freshest produce you can find—it really does make a difference here.

2 tablespoons extra-virgin olive oil

1 red onion, thinly sliced

2 medium zucchini, diced

1 pint cherry or grape tomatoes, halved

2 garlic cloves, smashed

¼ cup dry white wine

4 boneless, skinless chicken thighs

1 teaspoon herbes de Provence

Sea salt

Freshly ground black pepper

½ cup coarsely chopped fresh basil

PER SERVING
Calories: 251;
Fat: 12g;
Saturated Fat: 2g;
Sodium: 112mg;
Total Carbohydrates: 11g;
Net Carbohydrates: 8g;
Fiber: 3g;
Sugar: 6g;
Protein: 24g

1. Preheat the oven to 400°F.
2. Heat a large oven-safe skillet over medium-high heat until hot, then pour in the oil, and tilt to coat the bottom.
3. Add the onion, and sauté for 2 to 3 minutes, or until barely softened.
4. Add the zucchini, and sauté for 1 to 2 minutes, or until just browned.
5. Stir in the tomatoes, garlic, and wine, and give everything a good toss.
6. Coat the chicken thighs with the herbes de Provence, and season with salt and pepper. Add them to the skillet, then transfer the pan to the oven, and roast for 15 minutes, or until the chicken is cooked through and the vegetables are gently browned and bubbling.
7. Garnish with the basil right before serving.

VARIATION TIP: Want even more healthy vegetables in this recipe? I recommend adding eggplant and asparagus along with the zucchini.

Panfried Chicken Cordon Bleu

GLUTEN-FREE, SOY-FREE

Serves 4 | **PREP TIME:** 10 minutes | **COOK TIME:** 20 minutes

This riff on chicken cordon bleu replaces the bread crumbs with almond flour. It's a cinch to make, and at only 432 calories per serving, it fits into a healthy diet despite its decadent reputation.

4 boneless, skinless
   chicken breasts

4 slices deli ham

4 slices Swiss cheese

1 large egg

1 cup almond flour

1 teaspoon sea salt

1 teaspoon freshly ground
   black pepper

2 tablespoons coconut oil or
   extra-virgin olive oil

PER SERVING
Calories: 432;
Fat: 26g;
Saturated Fat: 13g;
Sodium: 983mg;
Total Carbohydrates: 6g;
Net Carbohydrates: 4g;
Fiber: 2g;
Sugar: 1g;
Protein: 43g

1. Carefully slice the chicken breasts in half horizontally nearly all the way through. One side should remain attached.
2. Unfold each chicken breast, and place 1 slice of ham and 1 slice of cheese into each.
3. Fold the chicken breasts closed, using a wooden toothpick to secure.
4. In a shallow bowl, whisk the egg.
5. In another shallow bowl, combine the almond flour, salt, and pepper.
6. Dip each stuffed chicken breast into the egg, then dredge in the almond flour mixture.
7. Heat a large skillet over medium-high heat until hot, then pour in the oil, and tilt to coat the bottom.
8. Add the chicken, and panfry for about 8 minutes on each side, or until cooked through and the cheese is melted.

COOKING TIP: This dish can also be made in the oven if you prefer. Bake for 20 to 25 minutes in an oven preheated to 400°F.

Shredded Chicken Tacos

DAIRY-FREE, GLUTEN-FREE, NUT-FREE, SOY-FREE

Serves 4 | **PREP TIME:** 10 minutes | **COOK TIME:** 15 minutes

The filling for these tacos can be used in so many different ways! Add it to soups and stews, serve it atop cauliflower rice with a generous dollop of guacamole, or use it to fill individual lettuce cups, as I've done here.

8 garlic cloves, minced

1 tablespoon chili powder

1 tablespoon smoked paprika

1 teaspoon ground cumin

1 teaspoon sea salt

2 tablespoons extra-virgin olive oil, divided

6 skinless chicken thighs

1 (15-ounce) can crushed tomatoes

1 tablespoon red-wine vinegar

8 butter lettuce leaves

½ cup sour cream

1 medium avocado, pitted, peeled, and thinly sliced

½ small red onion, thinly sliced

PER SERVING
Calories: 459;
Fat: 27g;
Saturated Fat: 7g;
Sodium: 863mg;
Total Carbohydrates: 18 g;
Net Carbohydrates: 9g;
Fiber: 9g;
Sugar: 7g;
Protein: 38g

1. To make the spice paste, put the garlic, chili powder, paprika, cumin, and salt into a mortar and pestle. Bash until the mixture forms a paste, adding 1 tablespoon of oil as you go. (If you don't have a mortar and pestle, you could also make this in a food processor. Be careful not to overprocess.)

2. Spread the spice paste over the chicken thighs. You can do this up to one day in advance, if you like.

3. Heat a large skillet over medium-high heat until hot, then pour in the remaining 1 tablespoon of oil, and tilt to coat the bottom.

4. Add the chicken, and sear for about 2 minutes on each side.

5. Add the tomatoes, and simmer for about 10 minutes, or until some of the liquid evaporates and the sauce begins to thicken.

6. Stir in the vinegar, then remove from the heat, and use 2 forks to shred the chicken.

7. To serve, divide the chicken filling among the lettuce cups, and top with sour cream and a few slices of avocado and red onion.

LEFTOVERS: The taco filling freezes really well. Just portion it out, seal it in zip-top plastic freezer bags, then defrost whenever you're ready to serve. To reheat, place in a small skillet over medium-low heat just until the meat is heated through.

Grilled Chicken Skewers with Thai Peanut Sauce

DAIRY-FREE

Serves 2 | **PREP TIME:** 10 minutes | **COOK TIME:** 10 minutes

Peanut sauce has to be one of the most addictive substances known to humanity. Like all of Thai cuisine, it's beautifully balanced between salty, sour, sweet, and savory flavors. This sauce works for lettuce wraps, too, so make a double batch, and store it in your refrigerator for when hunger strikes. If you're having trouble integrating the peanut sauce, place all of the ingredients in a large cup and use an immersion blender.

1½ pounds boneless, skinless chicken thighs, cut into 1½-inch pieces

1 tablespoon canola oil

Sea salt

Freshly ground black pepper

⅓ cup natural peanut butter

Juice of 1 lime

1 tablespoon soy sauce

1 teaspoon minced fresh ginger

1 teaspoon minced garlic

1 teaspoon sambal oelek or pinch red pepper flakes

2 or 3 drops liquid stevia

⅓ cup warm water

1. Preheat a gas grill to medium-high, fire up a charcoal grill, or set a heavy grill pan over medium-high heat on the stovetop.
2. Thread the chicken thighs onto 8 bamboo skewers. Brush with the oil, then season with salt and pepper.
3. Put the chicken on the grill, and sear for 5 minutes on each side, or until cooked through and gently browned.
4. Meanwhile, to make the peanut sauce, in a medium bowl, whisk the peanut butter with the lime juice, soy sauce, ginger, garlic, sambal oelek, and liquid stevia. Slowly drizzle in the water, whisking constantly.
5. Serve the chicken skewers with the peanut sauce on the side.

PER SERVING
Calories: 568;
Fat: 43g;
Saturated Fat: 10g;
Sodium: 496mg;
Total Carbohydrates: 10g;
Net Carbohydrates: 7g;
Fiber: 3g;
Sugar: 3g;
Protein: 44g

Chicken with Port, Mushrooms, and Cream

GLUTEN-FREE, NUT-FREE, SOY-FREE

Serves 2 | **PREP TIME:** 10 minutes | **COOK TIME:** 20 minutes

I wrote this recipe nearly a decade ago for a recipe contest that required five ingredients or fewer and featured chicken. I opted for chicken thighs, because they're richer in flavor than breasts. I also picked mushrooms, port, and cream, a classic French combination. Once you taste it, you'll discover why it won the competition!

1 tablespoon extra-virgin olive oil

4 boneless, skinless chicken thighs

Sea salt

Freshly ground black pepper

2 cups sliced cremini or button mushrooms

1 shallot, minced

2 tablespoons port

¼ cup heavy cream

PER SERVING
Calories: 325;
Fat: 20g;
Saturated Fat: 6g;
Sodium: 277mg;
Total Carbohydrates: 4g;
Net Carbohydrates: 3g;
Fiber: 1g;
Sugar: 1g;
Protein: 36g

1. Heat a large skillet over medium-high heat until hot, then pour in the oil, and tilt to coat the bottom.
2. Pat the chicken dry with paper towels, then season generously with salt and pepper.
3. Add the chicken to the skillet, and sear for 4 to 5 minutes.
4. Flip, and sear for 4 minutes. Transfer the chicken to a cutting board to rest.
5. Add the mushrooms to the skillet, and sear for about 2 minutes, or until gently browned.
6. Flip, and cook for 1 minute.
7. Add the shallot, and cook for 2 minutes.
8. Add the port, and cook, scraping the browned bits from the bottom, for about 2 minutes, or until it has mostly evaporated.
9. Add the heavy cream along with the chicken and any accumulated juices, then cook for 2 minutes.

Soy-Ginger Chicken and Squash Noodle Bowls

DAIRY-FREE, NUT-FREE

Serves 4 | **PREP TIME:** 5 minutes | **COOK TIME:** 25 minutes

Spaghetti squash is a staple in low-carb cooking because it's a pretty decent stand-in for pasta. Bonus: Because it's a vegetable, it comes packed with good-for-you nutrients, including fiber, vitamin C, manganese, and vitamin B_6. Paired with broccoli, sesame seeds, and chicken, it makes for a pretty healthy meal that's perfect for a family dinner or prepping ahead for a week of meals.

1 tablespoon sesame oil

1 pound boneless, skinless chicken thighs, cut into 2-inch pieces

1 pound broccoli florets

1 teaspoon minced fresh ginger

1 teaspoon minced garlic

1 teaspoon sambal oelek or another chili paste

¼ cup soy sauce

2 tablespoons freshly squeezed lime juice

1 Baked Spaghetti Squash (page 28)

2 tablespoons sesame seeds

PER SERVING
Calories: 306;
Fat: 17g;
Saturated Fat: 4g;
Sodium: 875mg;
Total Carbohydrates: 20g;
Net Carbohydrates: 15g;
Fiber: 5g;
Sugar: 3g;
Protein: 25g

1. Heat a large skillet over medium-high heat until hot, then pour in the oil, and tilt to coat the bottom.

2. Pat the chicken dry with paper towels, then add to the skillet, and sear for 4 to 5 minutes.

3. Flip, and sear for 4 minutes. Transfer to a bowl.

4. Add the broccoli to the skillet, and cook for 2 to 3 minutes, or until beginning to brown.

5. Add a few tablespoons of water, cover, and steam for 2 to 3 minutes, or until the broccoli is crisp-tender.

6. Add the ginger and garlic, and cook for about 30 seconds, or until fragrant.

7. Add the sambal oelek, soy sauce, and lime juice along with the chicken and any accumulated juices, and cook for about 1 minute.

8. Divide the spaghetti squash among 4 serving dishes, and top with the chicken and broccoli. Sprinkle each dish with about ½ tablespoon of sesame seeds.

INGREDIENT TIP: Ideally, use low-sodium soy sauce. It has more flavor and less salt than traditional versions. Also, pick a gluten-free option if you follow a gluten-free diet.

Chicken Thighs with Fennel and Sausage

DAIRY-FREE, GLUTEN-FREE, NUT-FREE, SOY-FREE

Serves 4 | **PREP TIME:** 5 minutes | **COOK TIME:** 25 minutes

With its fragrant ground fennel, spicy red pepper flakes, and fresh herbs, hot Italian sausage brings so much flavor to this one-pan dinner. I'm also upping the fennel flavor with fresh fennel bulb. If you haven't cooked with it before, give it a try. It has a tender, succulent texture that absorbs the olive oil and flavors from the sausage and gets tasty crispy bits when roasted. To prepare it, slice off the tough end of the root (only remove about ⅛ of an inch), then cut the fennel bulb vertically into four wedges, and remove the core. For a larger bulb, slice each quarter into two or three smaller wedges. They should still hold together at the bottom.

4 bone-in, skin-on
  chicken thighs
2 fennel bulbs, cored and cut
  into 1-inch wedges
4 hot Italian sausages, cut into
  2-inch pieces
2 tablespoons extra-virgin
  olive oil
Sea salt
Freshly ground black pepper

PER SERVING
Calories: 382;
Fat: 24g;
Saturated Fat: 7g;
Sodium: 598mg;
Total Carbohydrates: 10g;
Net Carbohydrates: 6g;
Fiber: 4g;
Sugar: 0g;
Protein: 34g

1. Preheat the oven to 400°F. Line a baking dish with parchment paper.
2. Place the chicken thighs skin-side up in the baking dish.
3. Arrange the fennel and sausage around the chicken. Drizzle with the oil, then season with salt and pepper.
4. Transfer the baking dish to the oven, and bake for 25 minutes, or until the chicken is cooked through.

COOKING TIP: Use a large, but not too large, baking dish—about 8-by-10 inches is good. This will allow some air to flow around the ingredients for increased browning, but keeps the foods close enough together that they won't dry out.

Chicken Thighs in Bacon-Mustard Cream Sauce

GLUTEN-FREE, NUT-FREE, SOY-FREE

Serves 4 | **PREP TIME:** 5 minutes | **COOK TIME:** 25 minutes

Bacon is a favorite among those following a low-carb lifestyle because it imparts a smoky-sweet flavor to recipes. I use it a bit more judiciously when I want to make an especially rich or decadent meal. This smoky, creamy sauce transforms everyday chicken and will become a fast favorite. It goes especially well with Oven-Roasted Brussels Sprouts (page 30).

4 bone-in, skin-on
   chicken thighs
1 tablespoon extra-virgin
   olive oil
Sea salt
Freshly ground black pepper
1 slice applewood-smoked
   bacon, diced
1 shallot, minced
1 teaspoon fresh thyme
¼ cup heavy cream
1 teaspoon Dijon mustard

PER SERVING
Calories: 245;
Fat: 18g;
Saturated Fat: 6g;
Sodium: 243mg;
Total Carbohydrates:
Net Carbohydrates: 1g;
Fiber: 0g;
Sugar: 0g;
Protein: 21g

1. Preheat the oven to 400°F. Line a baking dish with parchment paper.
2. Pat the chicken dry with paper towels, then coat with the oil, and season generously with salt and pepper.
3. Place the chicken skin-side up in the baking dish, and bake for 25 minutes, or until cooked through.
4. Meanwhile, heat a small skillet over medium heat, add the bacon, and cook for 10 minutes. It should render fat slowly as it crisps.
5. Add the shallot and thyme, and cook for 2 minutes.
6. Stir in the heavy cream and Dijon mustard, and cook for 2 to 3 minutes, or until the sauce thickens. Season with salt and pepper.
7. To serve, spread a generous spoonful of the cream sauce over each plate, and top with the chicken.

VARIATION TIP: If you prefer a slightly lighter option, use 2 boneless, skinless chicken breasts instead of the chicken thighs.

Pancetta and Tomato Roasted Chicken with Mozzarella

GLUTEN-FREE, NUT-FREE, SOY-FREE

Serves 4 | **PREP TIME:** 5 minutes | **COOK TIME:** 20 minutes

This recipe brings all of the tasty flavors of pizza together in a one-dish entrée—without the carbs. The fresh basil really livens up the dish, so don't skip it. Pancetta is Italian salt-cured pork belly. If you can't find it, uncured bacon is also fine. Fresh mozzarella is ideal because it has a softer texture than the shredded or block mozzarella, but use whatever is convenient.

4 ounces pancetta

4 medium boneless, skinless chicken breasts (about 6 ounces each)

Sea salt

Freshly ground black pepper

1 pint grape tomatoes

1 tablespoon fresh oregano or 1 teaspoon dried oregano

1 cup coarsely chopped fresh basil

8 ounces fresh mozzarella cheese, hand torn into bite-size pieces

PER SERVING
Calories: 450;
Fat: 24g;
Saturated Fat: 10g;
Sodium: 1133mg;
Total Carbohydrates: 6g;
Net Carbohydrates: 5g;
Fiber: 1g;
Sugar: 2g;
Protein: 53g

1. Preheat the oven to 425°F.
2. Heat a cast-iron or other oven-safe skillet over medium heat until hot.
3. Put the pancetta in the skillet, and cook for about 3 minutes, or until it renders just enough fat to coat the bottom.
4. Pat the chicken dry with paper towels, and season generously with salt and pepper.
5. Push the pancetta to the sides of the skillet, then add the chicken, and sear for 3 minutes.
6. Flip the chicken, and add the tomatoes and oregano, stirring around the chicken.
7. Transfer the skillet to the oven, and roast for 12 minutes.
8. Scatter the basil over the dish, followed by the mozzarella cheese, and return to the oven for 2 minutes, or just until the cheese is bubbling.

VARIATION TIP: Feel free to add your other favorite pizza toppings, such as olives, bell peppers, and onions at the same time as the tomatoes.

Chorizo Chicken with Salsa Verde

GLUTEN-FREE, NUT-FREE, SOY-FREE

Serves 4 | **PREP TIME:** 5 minutes | **COOK TIME:** 25 minutes

Seasoned with dried chiles, garlic, oregano, cloves, and vinegar, chorizo imparts so much flavor and complexity to this one-pan chicken dish. Choose uncured, raw chorizo, which you can find in the meat section or frozen section of well-stocked grocery stores or in Latino markets. It is a complete meal on its own, or serve with Cauli Rice (page 29).

4 ounces chorizo, casings removed, crumbled

4 medium boneless, skinless chicken breasts (about 6 ounces each)

Sea salt

Freshly ground black pepper

1 green bell pepper, thinly sliced

1 red bell pepper, thinly sliced

½ onion, thinly sliced

1 jalapeño pepper, stemmed and seeded

1 bunch fresh cilantro, coarsely chopped

2 garlic cloves, smashed

1 tablespoon freshly squeezed lime juice

⅓ cup extra-virgin olive oil

PER SERVING
Calories: 480;
Fat: 30g;
Saturated Fat: 7g;
Sodium: 524mg;
Total Carbohydrates: 7g;
Net Carbohydrates: 6g;
Fiber: 1g;
Sugar: 3g;
Protein: 47g

1. Preheat the oven to 425°F.
2. Heat a cast-iron or other oven-safe skillet over medium heat until hot.
3. Add the chorizo, and cook for about 3 minutes, or until it renders just enough fat to coat the bottom.
4. Pat the chicken dry with paper towels, and season generously with salt and pepper.
5. Push the chorizo to the sides of the skillet, then add the chicken, and sear for 3 minutes.
6. Flip the chicken, and add the bell peppers and onion to the skillet, stirring around the chicken.
7. Transfer the skillet to the oven, and roast for 15 minutes, or until the chicken is cooked through and the vegetables are gently browned and tender.
8. Meanwhile, to make the salsa verde, put the jalapeño, cilantro, garlic, lime juice, and oil in a blender, and purée until mostly smooth, scraping down the sides as needed. Season with salt and pepper.
9. Divide the chicken and vegetables among 4 serving plates, and serve with the salsa verde on the side.

Seared Strip Steak Salad with Gorgonzola and Roasted Red Peppers, page 66

4

pork, beef, and lamb

Everything Pizza with Cauliflower Crust

GLUTEN-FREE, SOY-FREE

Serves 4 | **PREP TIME:** 5 minutes | **COOK TIME:** 25 minutes

This pizza packs a lot of veggies into each bite. The crust is made of cauliflower, and it's topped with bell pepper, mushrooms, and olives. But it still has all the familiar pizza flavors you love—melty mozzarella and spicy pepperoni. To make this a vegetarian pie, grab some Beyond Meat Hot Italian Sausages instead of the pepperoni. They are surprisingly close to the real deal, with fennel seed, spicy red chile peppers, and just the right amount of fat to make them indulgent.

1 medium head cauliflower, cored and coarsely chopped

½ teaspoon sea salt

1 large egg

½ cup grated Parmesan cheese

½ cup almond flour

2 tablespoons coconut flour

1 tablespoon Italian herb blend

1 cup marinara sauce

8 ounces shredded mozzarella cheese

4 ounces thinly sliced uncured pepperoni

½ cup thinly sliced bell pepper (any color)

¼ cup thinly sliced black olives

½ cup thinly sliced button mushrooms

1. Preheat the oven to 425°F. Line a pizza pan or a rimmed baking sheet with a large square of parchment paper.

2. Run the cauliflower through a food processor fitted with the grater attachment. (Or grate it on a box grater using the largest holes.) Transfer to a glass or ceramic (not metal) baking dish, and season with the salt.

3. Microwave the cauliflower on high for 3 minutes. (If you don't have a microwave, place in a steamer basket set over ½-inch of simmering water, and steam for 5 minutes.) Fluff with a fork and let cool until it's comfortable to the touch.

4. Place the cauliflower in a clean kitchen towel, and wring as much moisture from it as you can. Try to get it really dry. Transfer to a large mixing bowl.

5. Add the egg, Parmesan cheese, almond flour, coconut flour, and herb blend. Mix thoroughly.

PER SERVING
Calories: 499;
Fat: 32g;
Saturated Fat: 14g;
Sodium: 1627mg;
Total Carbohydrates: 22g;
Net Carbohydrates: 12g;
Fiber: 10g;
Sugar: 7g;
Protein: 35g

6. Spread the cauliflower crust mixture onto the pizza pan in a very thin layer, about 1/8-inch thick.

7. Transfer the pan to the oven, and bake for 8 to 10 minutes, or until the crust is gently browned.

8. Scatter the marinara sauce, mozzarella cheese, pepperoni, bell pepper, olives, and mushrooms over the pizza.

9. Return the pizza pan to the oven, and bake for another 8 to 10 minutes, or until the cheese is bubbling.

INGREDIENT TIP: Choose a marinara sauce with no added sugar, especially if it comes in the form of high-fructose corn syrup.

Oktoberfest Brats and Cabbage

DAIRY-FREE, GLUTEN-FREE, NUT-FREE, SOY-FREE

Serves 4 | **PREP TIME:** 5 minutes | **COOK TIME:** 15 to 20 minutes

My husband grew up in Germany, and when we visited his parents there, I was eager to savor the country's cuisine. One of my favorite German dishes was bratwurst. It's often served without a bun on a bed of sauerkraut and eaten with a knife and fork—making it low-carb friendly. Here I pair it with roasted cabbage, a staple vegetable in German cooking, and spicy mustard.

½ head green cabbage, cored and coarsely chopped

2 tablespoons extra-virgin olive oil

Sea salt

Freshly ground black pepper

8 bratwursts (about 1½ pounds total)

1 teaspoon apple cider vinegar

Spicy German mustard, for serving

1. Preheat the oven to 350°F.
2. Place the cabbage in a baking dish, and drizzle with the oil. Season generously with salt and pepper.
3. Place the bratwursts on top of the cabbage.
4. Transfer the baking dish to the oven, and bake for 15 to 18 minutes, or until the bratwursts are cooked through.
5. Drizzle the vinegar into the cabbage, and toss gently to mix.
6. Serve the bratwursts and cabbage with mustard on the side.

PER SERVING
Calories: 684;
Fat: 57g;
Saturated Fat: 19g;
Sodium: 1675mg;
Total Carbohydrates: 9g;
Net Carbohydrates: 7g;
Fiber: 2g;
Sugar: 3g;
Protein: 29g

VARIATION TIP: Apple cider vinegar is one kind of acid you can use to brighten the flavor of any dish. Other options are lemon juice and red-wine or white-wine vinegars.

Ginger Pork Lettuce Cups with Pickled Red Onion

DAIRY-FREE, GLUTEN-FREE, NUT-FREE, SOY-FREE

Serves 4 | **PREP TIME:** 10 minutes | **COOK TIME:** 15 minutes

Fragrant ginger, pungent garlic, and spicy red pepper flakes make the pork in these lettuce cups especially tasty. Top them off with quick-pickled red onion, carrots, and cilantro for a healthy, colorful meal. The red-wine vinegar mellows the intensity of the onion and brightens the entire dish, so don't skip the pickling.

½ small red onion, thinly sliced

2 tablespoons red-wine vinegar

Sea salt

1 tablespoon coconut oil

1 tablespoon minced
    fresh ginger

1 tablespoon minced garlic

Pinch red pepper flakes

1½ pounds ground pork

Freshly ground black pepper

1 head butter lettuce, leaves
    separated

2 carrots, cut into thin
    matchsticks

1 cup coarsely chopped fresh
    cilantro

1. To make the quick-pickled onion, put the onion in a medium bowl, and toss with the vinegar. Season with salt.

2. Heat a large skillet over medium-high heat until hot, then melt the coconut oil, and tilt to coat the bottom.

3. Add the ginger, garlic, and red pepper flakes, and cook for about 30 seconds, or just until fragrant.

4. Add the pork, and sauté for 7 to 8 minutes, or until just cooked through. Season with salt and pepper.

5. To serve, divide the cooked pork among the lettuce leaves. Top with some carrots, cilantro, and quick-pickled onion.

LEFTOVERS: You may find that you like these quick-pickled onions so much that you'll want to add them to everything. So make a double batch, and store leftovers in a covered container in the refrigerator for up to a week.

PER SERVING
Calories: 413;
Fat: 28g;
Saturated Fat: 12g;
Sodium: 212mg;
Total Carbohydrates: 9g;
Net Carbohydrates: 7g;
Fiber: 2g;
Sugar: 3g;
Protein: 31g

Roasted Pork Tenderloin with Apple-Cabbage Slaw

DAIRY-FREE, GLUTEN-FREE, NUT-FREE, SOY-FREE

Serves 4 | **PREP TIME:** 10 minutes | **COOK TIME:** 20 minutes

Apples in a low-carb cookbook? Yes, you read that right. Here's why I chose to include them: One medium apple has 25 grams of carbs, and five of those are fiber. When you divide that into four portions, it's a measly 5 grams of net carbs per serving. Moreover, apples contain soluble fiber, and the peel is a good source of chromium, a mineral that improves insulin sensitivity.

2 tablespoons canola oil, divided

1 (1¼-pound) boneless pork tenderloin

Sea salt

Freshly ground black pepper

1 tablespoon minced fresh rosemary

1 Granny Smith apple, cored and cut into 8 wedges

½ head red cabbage, cored and thinly sliced

½ red onion, thinly sliced

1 tablespoon apple cider vinegar

½ cup coarsely chopped fresh flat-leaf parsley

PER SERVING
Calories: 263;
Fat: 11g;
Saturated Fat: 2g;
Sodium: 271mg;
Total Carbohydrates: 15g;
Net Carbohydrates: 10g;
Fiber: 5g;
Sugar: 9g;
Protein: 28g

1. Preheat the oven to 425°F.
2. Heat a large oven-safe skillet over medium-high heat until hot, then pour in 1 tablespoon of oil, and tilt to coat the bottom.
3. Pat the pork dry with paper towels, then season generously with salt, pepper, and the rosemary.
4. Add the pork to the skillet, and sear for about 10 minutes total, or until gently browned on all sides.
5. In a large bowl, toss the apple, cabbage, and onion with the remaining 1 tablespoon of oil. Scatter this around the pork in the skillet.
6. Transfer the skillet to the oven, and roast for 10 minutes, or until the pork is cooked through, and the vegetables are vibrant and crisp-tender.
7. Transfer the pork to a cutting board to rest.
8. Add the apple cider vinegar and parsley to the skillet, and toss gently to mix.
9. Slice the pork on a bias, and serve with the slaw.

INGREDIENT TIP: Apples are one of the more important fruits to purchase organic, because conventionally grown apples have significant pesticide residues. Once you start buying organic apples, you'll quickly notice a difference over conventional produce.

Swedish Meatballs

GLUTEN-FREE, SOY-FREE

Serves 4 | **PREP TIME:** 5 minutes | **COOK TIME:** 20 minutes

Most meatball recipes are loaded with fillers such as bread crumbs or rice, which means lots of carbs! This version uses almond flour and egg to bind the ingredients. Also, because the meatballs are prepared in a skillet with pan sauce instead of baked, they retain a lot of their moisture. They're especially tasty with the Celery Root Purée (page 27).

8 ounces ground beef

8 ounces ground pork

1 large egg

1 cup grated onion

2 garlic cloves, minced

¼ cup almond flour

1 teaspoon sea salt

½ teaspoon freshly ground
  black pepper

¼ teaspoon ground nutmeg

⅛ teaspoon ground allspice

1 tablespoon canola oil

1 cup low-sodium beef broth

¼ cup dry white wine

2 tablespoons cold butter

½ cup sour cream

PER SERVING
Calories: 402;
Fat: 31g;
Saturated Fat: 13g;
Sodium: 604mg;
Total Carbohydrates: 6g;
Net Carbohydrates: 5g;
Fiber: 1g;
Sugar: 2g;
Protein: 23g

1. In a large bowl, combine the beef, pork, egg, onion, garlic, almond flour, salt, pepper, nutmeg, and allspice. Mix with your hands until just combined, then form into 8 meatballs.

2. Heat a large deep skillet over medium-high heat until hot, then pour in the oil, and tilt to coat the bottom.

3. Add the meatballs, and sear for about 2 minutes, or until gently browned on one side.

4. Turn the meatballs, and brown another side for about 2 minutes, then turn again to brown on a third side for 2 minutes.

5. Add the beef broth and white wine, then bring to a gentle simmer, and cook for 8 to 10 minutes, or until the meatballs are cooked through and about half the liquid has evaporated. Transfer the meatballs to a serving platter.

6. Whisk the cold butter and sour cream into the sauce in the skillet, and cook over low heat for about 1 more minute, or just until integrated into the sauce. Pour over the meatballs and serve.

COOKING TIP: Whisking cold butter into a pan sauce that contains wine or another acid is a classic French technique that produces rich, tangy sauces. The acid in the wine interacts with the milk solids in the butter, suspending them in the liquid.

Cheesy Meatball Casserole

NUT-FREE, SOY-FREE

Serves 8 | **PREP TIME:** 5 minutes | **COOK TIME:** 25 minutes

With plenty of meaty and cheesy goodness, this casserole is the kind of food that should come to mind when you think "low-carb diet." Not only is it rich and delicious, it's also easy—sometimes it's nice to have a recipe that's really more about assembly than about cooking. You simply throw all the ingredients into a baking dish, put it in the oven, and wait for a delicious dinner.

1 (32-ounce) jar marinara sauce

1 (32-ounce) package frozen Italian meatballs

8 ounces shredded mozzarella cheese

1 packed cup coarsely chopped fresh basil

¼ cup grated Parmesan cheese

PER SERVING
Calories: 327;
Fat: 24g;
Saturated Fat: 10g;
Sodium: 1622mg;
Total Carbohydrates: 10g;
Net Carbohydrates: 8g;
Fiber: 2g;
Sugar: 7g;
Protein: 21g

1. Preheat the oven to 400°F.

2. Spread about 1 cup of the marinara sauce into an 8-by-10-inch baking dish.

3. Put the meatballs in the baking dish, and scatter the mozzarella cheese and basil on top.

4. Cover with the remaining marinara sauce.

5. Cover the baking dish tightly with foil, transfer to the oven, and bake for 20 minutes.

6. Remove and discard the foil, and top with the Parmesan.

7. Return the baking dish to the oven, and bake for 5 minutes, or until the cheese is melted and beginning to brown.

INGREDIENT TIP: Look for meatballs without a lot of added fillers, such as bread crumbs or rice. Fontanini Mamma Ranne offers a beef and pork meatball with only 2 grams of carbohydrates per serving.

Mexican Pacholas with Avocado Salsa

DAIRY-FREE, GLUTEN-FREE, NUT-FREE, SOY-FREE

Serves 4 | **PREP TIME:** 15 minutes | **COOK TIME:** 10 minutes

Pacholas—patties or tortillas made from seasoned ground meat—are very popular in the west-central regions of Mexico among kids and home cooks looking for a quick and simple meal. It's easy to see why; they take about as much work as frying up a burger—and you'll never miss the bun!

2 large avocados, pitted, peeled, and diced

½ small red onion, thinly sliced

1 small jalapeño pepper, seeded and minced

1 pint grape tomatoes, halved

1 cup fresh corn kernels (from about 3 corn cobs)

½ cup minced fresh cilantro

2 tablespoons lime juice

Sea salt

8 ounces ground beef

8 ounces ground pork

2 teaspoons ancho chili powder

1 teaspoon dried oregano

1 teaspoon ground cumin

3 garlic cloves, minced

½ teaspoon sea salt

⅛ teaspoon freshly ground black pepper

2 tablespoons canola oil

1. To make the salsa, in a large mixing bowl, combine the avocados, onion, jalapeño pepper, tomatoes, corn, cilantro, and lime juice. Season with salt.

2. In another large mixing bowl, combine the beef, pork, chili powder, oregano, cumin, garlic, salt, and pepper. Divide into 4 equal portions.

3. Place each portion on a sheet of parchment paper. Top each with a second sheet of parchment paper, and use a rolling pin to form roughly ⅛-inch-thick patties.

4. Heat a large skillet over medium-high heat until hot, then pour in the oil, and tilt to coat the bottom.

5. Carefully peel off the top sheets of parchment paper. Working in 2 batches, transfer the patties to the skillet. Cook for about 2 minutes on each side, or until just cooked through. Press on the center of each pachola; it should feel firm but slightly springy. Don't overcook. Transfer to a cutting board to rest.

6. To serve, place each pachola on a serving plate, and top with the salsa.

PER SERVING
Calories: 484;
Fat: 35g;
Saturated Fat: 7g;
Sodium: 168mg;
Total Carbohydrates: 23g;
Net Carbohydrates: 13g;
Fiber: 10g;
Sugar: 5g;
Protein: 26g

INGREDIENT TIP: Frozen and defrosted corn kernels are fine if corn isn't in season. Look for fire-roasted corn for even more flavor.

Skillet Cottage Pie with Cauliflower Mash

GLUTEN-FREE, NUT-FREE, SOY-FREE

Serves 4 | **PREP TIME:** 10 minutes | **COOK TIME:** 20 minutes

Traditional cottage pie is covered in a thick layer of mashed potatoes. In this recipe, I lighten things up with mashed cauliflower. You can add one russet potato to the mix, or use cauliflower only, as I've done here. Given the richly flavored filling, you may not even notice the difference.

1 large head cauliflower, cored and cut into florets

1 tablespoon sea salt

2 tablespoons butter

1 tablespoon canola oil

1 onion, finely diced

2 carrots, finely diced

1 stalk celery, finely diced

1 tablespoon minced fresh rosemary

1 teaspoon minced fresh thyme

Sea salt

1 pound ground beef

1 tablespoon tomato paste

¼ cup dry red wine

Freshly ground black pepper

PER SERVING
Calories: 337;
Fat: 17g;
Saturated Fat: 7g;
Sodium: 278mg;
Total Carbohydrates: 19g;
Net Carbohydrates: 11g;
Fiber: 8g;
Sugar: 8g;
Protein: 27g

1. Put the cauliflower in a large pot, and season with the salt. Fill the pot with water so that it covers the cauliflower by 1 inch. Cover, bring to a boil, and cook for 15 minutes, or until tender.

2. Drain the cauliflower thoroughly, and transfer to a food processor. Add the butter, and purée until smooth.

3. While the cauliflower is cooking, heat a large cast-iron skillet over medium-high heat until hot, then pour in the oil, and tilt to coat the bottom.

4. Add the onion, carrots, celery, rosemary, thyme, and a generous pinch sea salt, then cook for 5 minutes, or until the vegetables begin to soften.

5. Push the vegetables to the sides of the skillet, and place the ground beef in the center of the pan. Break up the meat with a spoon, and cook for about 5 minutes, or until no pink remains.

6. Add the tomato paste and wine, then bring to a simmer, and cook for 2 minutes to allow the alcohol to cook off. Season with salt and pepper.

7. Preheat the broiler to high, and place a rack near the top of the oven.

8. Spread the mashed cauliflower on top of the meat mixture in the skillet. Place under the broiler for 2 to 3 minutes, or until the top is gently browned.

Chimichurri Grilled Steak

DAIRY-FREE, GLUTEN-FREE, NUT-FREE, SOY-FREE

Serves 6 | **PREP TIME:** 5 minutes | **COOK TIME:** 10 minutes

Grassy parsley, pungent garlic, and tangy red-wine vinegar liven up grilled steak in this classic Argentine recipe. I'm partial to fresh herbs, but dried oregano retains its flavor and is a common ingredient in traditional chimichurri—plus, it's easy to find, making this an excellent weeknight staple. Serve with Avocado-Citrus Salad (page 24). Mild Fresno chiles are available in most grocery stores, but if you can't find one, you can use half a jalapeño pepper instead, which is a bit hotter.

2 cups minced fresh
   flat-leaf parsley

1 tablespoon dried oregano

2 to 3 tablespoons
   minced garlic

1 Fresno chile, seeded
   and minced

1 cup extra-virgin olive oil

¼ cup red-wine vinegar

Sea salt

Freshly ground black pepper

2 pounds flank steak

1 tablespoon canola oil

PER SERVING
Calories: 403;
Fat: 29g;
Saturated Fat: 7g;
Sodium: 133mg;
Total Carbohydrates: 2g;
Net Carbohydrates: 1g;
Fiber: 1g;
Sugar: 0g;
Protein: 34g

1. In a medium bowl, to make the chimichurri, combine the parsley, oregano, garlic, chile, oil, and vinegar. Season with salt and pepper.

2. Preheat a gas grill to medium-high, fire up a charcoal grill, or set a heavy grill pan over medium-high heat on the stovetop.

3. Pat the steak dry with paper towels, and coat with the oil. Season with salt and pepper.

4. Put the steak on the grill, and cook for about 4 minutes on each side, or until barely charred and still red in the center.

5. Cut the steak on the bias into thin strips. Serve with the chimichurri on the side.

INGREDIENT TIP: You might be tempted to reach for jarred garlic in this recipe. I don't blame you, but I don't recommend it. The flavor is distinctly different from fresh garlic, especially when you're serving it raw. So grab a handy silicone garlic peeler, and use fresh cloves.

Sizzling Steak Fajitas with Homemade Guacamole

DAIRY-FREE, GLUTEN-FREE, NUT-FREE, SOY-FREE

Serves 4 | **PREP TIME:** 10 minutes | **COOK TIME:** 15 minutes

When it comes to replacing corn and flour tortillas, you have a few options. You can go the lettuce wrap route; opt for a store-bought low-carb tortilla made with coconut flour, almond flour, or another substitute; or make your own. If you can, opt for homemade guacamole. It's easy and tastes so much better. This version makes about 2 cups.

For the guacamole

4 large ripe avocados, pitted
and peeled
Generous pinch kosher salt
1 garlic clove, minced
1 shallot, minced
1 tablespoon freshly squeezed
lime juice

For the fajitas

3 tablespoons canola
oil, divided
1 tablespoon chili powder
2 teaspoons ground coriander
2 teaspoons ground cumin
1 teaspoon sea salt, plus more
for seasoning
1 pound skirt steak
1 onion, thinly sliced
1 red bell pepper, thinly sliced
1 green bell pepper,
thinly sliced

TO MAKE THE GUACAMOLE

1. In a mortar and pestle or a small bowl, combine the avocados, salt, garlic, shallot, and lime juice, and mash until thoroughly integrated, adding more salt and lime juice as needed.

2. Store leftovers tightly covered in the refrigerator for up to 2 days.

TO MAKE THE FAJITAS

1. In a bowl, combine 2 tablespoons of oil, the chili powder, coriander, cumin, and 1 teaspoon salt, then coat the steak in the mixture.

2. Heat a cast-iron skillet over medium-high heat until hot.

3. Put the steak in the skillet, and sear on each side for about 4 minutes. Transfer to a cutting board to rest.

8 lettuce wraps or low-carb
  tortillas
1 cup homemade guacamole,
  or good-quality store-bought
  guacamole

PER SERVING
Calories: 547; Fat: 42g;
Saturated Fat: 9g;
Sodium: 710mg;
Total Carbohydrates: 19g;
Net Carbohydrates: 10g;
Fiber: 9g;
Sugar: 5g;
Protein: 28g

4. Pour in the remaining 1 tablespoon of oil to the skillet, then add the onion and bell peppers, and sauté for 5 minutes, or until vibrant and gently browned. Season with a pinch salt.

5. Thinly slice the steak. Serve with lettuce wraps or tortillas, with guacamole on the side.

COOKING TIP: You can coat the steak in the oil and spice mixture up to 24 hours ahead of time; keep the steak in a covered container in the refrigerator, and remove about 30 minutes before cooking.

Seared Strip Steak Salad with Gorgonzola and Roasted Red Peppers

GLUTEN-FREE, NUT-FREE, SOY-FREE

Serves 2 | **PREP TIME:** 10 minutes | **COOK TIME:** 15 minutes

With its generous portion of steak, rich Gorgonzola cheese, and luxurious wine reduction, this hefty salad belongs on your dinner table. It's naturally low in carbohydrates and is adapted from the first cookbook by one of my favorite celebrity chefs, Tyler Florence's Real Kitchen. I received the book when I got married and have cooked nearly every recipe in the years since; each page is marked with oil splatters and chocolate smears.

2 tablespoons extra-virgin
    olive oil, divided

2 (6-ounce) New York
    strip steaks

Sea salt

Freshly ground black pepper

2 fresh thyme sprigs

½ cup dry red wine

4 cups assorted salad greens,
    such as baby spinach, kale,
    and artisanal lettuces

Juice of ½ lemon

⅓ cup crumbled Gorgonzola
    cheese (2 ounces)

2 roasted red bell
    peppers, sliced

½ cup pitted Kalamata olives

1. Preheat the oven to 350°F.
2. Heat a medium oven-safe skillet over medium-high heat until hot, then pour in 1 tablespoon of oil, and tilt to coat the bottom.
3. Pat the steaks dry with paper towels, and season generously with salt and pepper.
4. Add the steaks to the skillet, and sear for 5 minutes.
5. Flip, and sear for 3 minutes.
6. Add the thyme, then transfer the skillet to the oven, and cook for 3 to 5 minutes for medium-rare.
7. Carefully return the skillet to the stovetop. Transfer the steaks to a cutting board to rest.
8. Add the wine to the skillet, and simmer over medium-low heat for about 3 minutes, or until reduced to about 3 tablespoons. Discard the thyme.
9. In a large bowl, toss the salad greens with the remaining 1 tablespoon of oil and the lemon juice, and divide between 2 serving plates.

PER SERVING
Calories: 570;
Fat: 32g;
Saturated Fat: 10g;
Sodium: 1062mg;
Total Carbohydrates: 16g;
Net Carbohydrates: 9g;
Fiber: 7g;
Sugar: 5g;
Protein: 48g

10. Scatter the Gorgonzola cheese, roasted peppers, and olives on top.

11. After the steaks have rested, slice them thinly on a bias, and arrange on top of the salad. Pour the wine reduction from the pan on top.

COOKING TIP: To prepare the bell peppers, cut them in half lengthwise, then remove the seeds, core, and membranes. Flatten the peppers with your hand, and lightly coat the skin side of the peppers with oil. Place them under a broiler preheated to high, and broil for 2 to 3 minutes, or until deeply charred. Transfer the peppers to a container, and cover tightly with a lid or plastic wrap. Let steam for 10 minutes, then carefully use your hands to peel away the charred skin, and discard it.

Seared Rib Eye with Mushrooms and Browned Butter

GLUTEN-FREE, NUT-FREE, SOY-FREE

Serves 4 | **PREP TIME:** 5 minutes | **COOK TIME:** 15 minutes

With just five ingredients (not counting the oil, salt, and pepper), this one-pan meal is as easy as it gets. Don't let that fool you though—it's really tasty. The secret is in the technique. A wicked hot pan creates a gorgeous browned crust on the steak, and sautéing the mushrooms brings out all of their umami goodness. Finally, browned butter brings a nutty richness to the dish, which is finished with fresh thyme for some herbal notes. Serve with Creamed Broccoli (page 34) and a full-bodied red wine for a decadent low-carb dinner.

1 (16-ounce) rib eye steak

1 tablespoon canola oil

Sea salt

Freshly ground black pepper

4 tablespoons (½ stick) butter

8 ounces cremini or button mushrooms, thickly sliced

1 teaspoon fresh thyme

1 teaspoon minced garlic

1. Preheat the oven to 350°F.
2. Heat a large cast-iron skillet over high heat until it is very hot, about 5 minutes.
3. Pat the steak dry with paper towels, then coat with the oil. Season generously with salt and pepper.
4. Put the steak in the skillet, and sear for 5 minutes.
5. Flip, and sear for 2 minutes.
6. Transfer the skillet to the oven, and cook for 2 to 3 minutes for medium-rare.
7. Carefully return the skillet to the stovetop. Transfer the steak to a cutting board to rest.
8. Add the butter to the skillet, and cook for 3 to 4 minutes, or until the foam has subsided and the solids begin to rest on the bottom.

PER SERVING
Calories: 340;
Fat: 25g;
Saturated Fat: 12g;
Sodium: 207mg;
Total Carbohydrates: 4g;
Net Carbohydrates: 3g;
Fiber: 1g;
Sugar: 1g;
Protein: 27g

9. Add the mushrooms, and cook for about 2 minutes, or until well browned.

10. Flip, and add the thyme and garlic. Cook for 1 minute, or until fragrant.

11. To serve, cut the steak on a bias, divide among 4 plates, and top with the mushrooms and browned butter. Try to avoid picking up the milk solids at the bottom of the pan. You can do this by carefully (use a potholder) tipping the pan and using a spoon to scoop the clarified butter from the top.

COOKING TIP: What is umami? Often called the fifth taste in addition to sweet, salty, sour, and bitter, umami is a savory flavor that activates your glutamate receptors. You can taste umami flavor in seared meats, broth, mushrooms, celery, and fermented foods.

Stir-Fried Beef and Broccoli with Cashews

DAIRY-FREE

Serves 4 | **PREP TIME:** 10 minutes | **COOK TIME:** 15 minutes

Chinese takeout—only better—is now available in the comfort of your own home with this easy stir-fry recipe. This riff on the traditional skips the cornstarch for a healthy, low-carb meal. Serve with Cauli Rice (page 29).

1 tablespoon canola oil

1 teaspoon toasted sesame oil

1 pound boneless sirloin steak, cut into paper-thin slices

1 tablespoon minced fresh ginger

1 tablespoon minced garlic

¼ teaspoon red pepper flakes

8 cups broccoli florets and coarsely chopped stems

¼ cup water

¼ cup soy sauce

2 tablespoons freshly squeezed lime juice

¼ cup coarsely chopped toasted cashews

PER SERVING
Calories: 308;
Fat: 13g;
Saturated Fat: 3g;
Sodium: 1015mg;
Total Carbohydrates: 17g;
Net Carbohydrates: 10g;
Fiber: 7g;
Sugar: 4g;
Protein: 32g

1. Heat a large skillet over high heat until hot, then pour in the canola and sesame oils, and tilt to coat the bottom.

2. Add the steak, and stir-fry for 4 to 5 minutes, or until just cooked through.

3. Reduce the heat to medium. Add the ginger, garlic, and red pepper flakes, and cook for 30 seconds, or until just fragrant. Be careful not to burn. Transfer to a dish.

4. Add the broccoli to the skillet, and stir-fry for 2 minutes, or until beginning to brown.

5. Carefully add the water, cover, reduce the heat to low, and cook for 5 minutes, or until the broccoli is tender.

6. Remove the lid, return the steak and any accumulated juices to the skillet, add the soy sauce and lime juice, and cook for 1 minute.

7. Transfer the steak and broccoli to a serving dish, and top with the toasted cashews.

COOKING TIP: Whenever you're cooking with garlic, be careful not to burn it. Excessively high heat, few other ingredients, and scant oil or other liquid in the pan can all speed up the cooking process, and take you from fragrant garlic to a burnt, stinky mess. Unlike with onions or other ingredients, there really is no coming back from burnt garlic.

Beef and Mushroom Stroganoff

GLUTEN-FREE, NUT-FREE, SOY-FREE

Serves 4 | **PREP TIME:** 10 minutes | **COOK TIME:** 15 minutes

Beef stroganoff is a Russian dish of sautéed beef in a tangy sour cream sauce. In the United States, it's often served with egg noodles. This low-carb version opts for a generous helping of savory mushrooms instead and gets a boost of flavor from brandy. If you don't have brandy, no worries; just use dry white wine instead.

1 tablespoon canola oil

1 pound rib eye steak, thinly sliced on a bias

1 onion, halved and thinly sliced

8 ounces cremini or button mushrooms, sliced

¼ cup brandy or dry white wine

¾ cup low-sodium beef broth or stock

1 teaspoon whole-grain mustard

½ cup sour cream

Sea salt

Freshly ground black pepper

¼ cup coarsely chopped fresh flat-leaf parsley

PER SERVING
Calories: 328;
Fat: 20g;
Saturated Fat: 9g;
Sodium: 267mg;
Total Carbohydrates: 8g;
Net Carbohydrates: 6g;
Fiber 2g;
Sugar: 2g;
Protein: 28g

1. Heat a large skillet over high heat until hot, then pour in the oil, and tilt to coat the bottom.

2. Add the steak, and sauté for 2 to 3 minutes, or just until cooked through. Transfer to a dish.

3. Add the onion and mushrooms, and cook for 5 minutes, or until tender.

4. Carefully add the brandy to deglaze the skillet, scraping up the browned bits from the bottom. Cook for 1 minute to let some of the alcohol evaporate.

5. Add the beef broth and mustard, bring to a simmer, and cook for 2 to 3 minutes, or until slightly reduced.

6. Return the beef to the skillet, and cook for 2 to 3 minutes.

7. Remove the skillet from the heat, and stir in the sour cream. Season with salt and pepper.

8. To serve, transfer the beef and mushrooms to a serving dish, and top with the parsley.

INGREDIENT TIP: What's the difference between broth and stock? Typically, not that much. However, the original definition is that broth is made with meat and bones, while stock is made solely with bones. To make a tasty beef stock, roast 1 or 2 pounds of beef bones at 350°F for 45 minutes, or until deeply browned. Transfer to a large pot, and add half an onion, 2 garlic cloves, and 1 sprig fresh thyme. Season with salt, and cover generously with fresh water. Simmer for 3 to 4 hours, or until rich and fragrant. Strain and freeze in smaller portions.

Laotian Ground Meat Lettuce Cups

DAIRY-FREE, GLUTEN-FREE, SOY-FREE

Serves 4 | **PREP TIME:** 5 minutes | **COOK TIME:** 10 minutes

Larb is a ground meat dish richly seasoned with chiles, lemongrass, fish sauce, and garlic. In addition to ground lamb or beef, the meat filling includes ground peanuts, which add a tasty textural element. Fish sauce is a pungent liquid used in Southeast Asian cooking to impart savory flavors in a wide array of dishes. Don't worry—it doesn't make food taste fishy. But a little goes a long way, so measure carefully. Find it in the international aisle in grocery stores, Asian markets, or online.

1 tablespoon canola oil

1 pound ground lamb or beef

½ small red onion, thinly sliced

1 tablespoon minced fresh
  lemongrass or ginger

1 tablespoon minced garlic

1 Thai chile, seeded and minced

½ cup finely chopped
  roasted peanuts

Juice of 1 lime

1 tablespoon fish sauce

¼ cup finely chopped
  fresh mint

8 Bibb lettuce leaves

1. Heat a large skillet over medium-high heat until hot, then pour in the oil, and tilt to coat the bottom.

2. Add the lamb, and sauté for about 5 minutes, or until nearly cooked through, breaking up the pieces as you go.

3. Add the onion, lemongrass, garlic, and chile, and cook for 1 minute, or until just fragrant.

4. Add the peanuts, lime juice, and fish sauce, and cook for 1 minute.

5. Remove the skillet from the heat, and stir in the mint.

6. To serve, divide the ground lamb mixture among the lettuce cups.

PER SERVING
Calories: 311;
Fat: 21g;
Saturated Fat: 5g;
Sodium: 439mg;
Total Carbohydrates: 6g;
Net Carbohydrates: 4g;
Fiber: 2g;
Sugar: 1g;
Protein: 28g

INGREDIENT TIP: Prepared lemongrass is often available alongside herbs in well-stocked grocery stores. To use fresh lemongrass, bash the base of the stalk with the broad side of a knife. Peel away the tough outer layers, and finely chop the bottom 2 inches of the stalk.

Roasted Eggplant with Ground Lamb and Pine Nuts

GLUTEN-FREE, SOY-FREE

Serves 4 | **PREP TIME:** 5 minutes | **COOK TIME:** 25 minutes

Many eggplant recipes require salting the eggplant ahead of time to draw out moisture and bitterness. I've tried this recipe both ways and find that the unsalted eggplant works even better to produce a silky texture and sublime caramelized flavor. Plus, it's faster! Top the low-carb vegetable with spiced ground lamb, whole-milk yogurt, and toasted pine nuts for a healthy low-carb meal.

2 medium eggplants, cut lengthwise into ½-inch-thick slices

5 tablespoons extra-virgin olive oil, divided

Sea salt

½ small red onion, minced

1 pound ground lamb

1 tablespoon tomato paste

1 teaspoon minced garlic

½ teaspoon ground cinnamon

⅛ teaspoon ground allspice

Freshly ground black pepper

½ cup whole-milk plain yogurt

¼ cup pine nuts

¼ cup minced fresh flat-leaf parsley

PER SERVING
Calories: 625;
Fat: 60g;
Saturated Fat: 16g;
Sodium: 103mg;
Total Carbohydrates: 20g;
Net Carbohydrates: 9g;
Fiber: 11g;
Sugar: 9g;
Protein: 24g

1. Preheat the oven to 375°F.
2. In a bowl, toss the eggplant with 4 tablespoons of oil, and spread onto a rimmed baking sheet. Season with salt.
3. Transfer the baking sheet to the oven, and bake for 25 minutes, or until gently browned and very soft.
4. Meanwhile, heat a large skillet over medium-high heat until hot, then pour in the remaining 1 tablespoon of oil, and tilt to coat the bottom. Add the onion, and cook for 3 minutes, or until beginning to soften.
5. Add the lamb, and cook for about 5 minutes, or until nearly cooked through. Add the tomato paste, and cook for 2 minutes, or until it begins to caramelize.
6. Add the garlic, cinnamon, and allspice, and season generously with salt and pepper. Cook for 1 minute, just to let the flavors come together.
7. To serve, arrange a couple slices of eggplant on each plate. Top with the ground lamb mixture. Drizzle with the yogurt, and sprinkle with pine nuts and parsley.

COOKING TIP: To toast pine nuts or other small nuts, seeds, and spices, place them in a dry skillet over medium heat. Gently shake the skillet back and forth for 2 to 3 minutes, or until the nuts are gently browned and fragrant.

*Shrimp Scampi,
page 85*

5

seafood

Smoked Salmon with Yogurt and Fennel

GLUTEN-FREE, NUT-FREE, SOY-FREE

Serves 4 | **PREP TIME:** 5 minutes

This recipe is perfect for a picnic or a light summer dinner. I love the contrast between the savory smoked salmon, the cool tanginess of the yogurt, and the bright crunch of the fennel. You could use another vegetable here if you're not keen on fennel; I recommend a mixture of cucumber and very thinly sliced red onion.

1 bulb fennel, cored and very finely sliced

Juice of 1 lime

1 cup whole-milk plain yogurt

1 small garlic clove, puréed

Pinch sea salt

1 pound sliced smoked salmon

Freshly ground black pepper

1. In a medium bowl, combine the fennel and lime juice.
2. In another bowl, whisk the yogurt, garlic, and salt.
3. To serve, divide the yogurt among 4 serving plates. Top with slices of smoked salmon and several pieces of fennel. Season with black pepper.

PER SERVING
Calories: 194;
Fat: 7g;
Saturated Fat: 2g;
Sodium: 2186mg;
Total Carbohydrates: 9g;
Net Carbohydrates: 6g;
Fiber: 3g;
Sugar: 3g;
Protein: 24g

Salmon Chowder

DAIRY-FREE, GLUTEN-FREE, NUT-FREE, SOY-FREE

Serves 4 | **PREP TIME:** 10 minutes | **COOK TIME:** 20 minutes

Growing up in the Pacific Northwest, salmon has been on my dinner table since before I can remember. Now, as an adult, salmon is my favorite fish, and this chowder showcases its depth of flavor. Layering fresh and smoked salmon really brings complexity and richness to the dish. Make sure to add the fresh herbs after you remove the soup from the heat, to keep their grassy freshness—the contrast really brightens the soup.

2 tablespoons extra-virgin olive oil

1 medium leek, white and light green parts only, rinsed thoroughly and thinly sliced

½ onion, diced

Sea salt

2 tablespoons tomato paste

Pinch red pepper flakes

½ cup dry white wine

4 cups vegetable broth or fish stock

1 pound wild-caught salmon fillets, cut into 2-inch pieces

1 cup heavy cream

4 ounces smoked salmon, broken into pieces

¼ cup minced fresh flat-leaf parsley

1 tablespoon minced fresh dill

PER SERVING
Calories: 640;
Fat: 49g;
Saturated Fat: 20g;
Sodium: 1428mg;
Total Carbohydrates: 11g;
Net Carbohydrates: 9g;
Fiber: 2g;
Sugar: 4g;
Protein: 33g

1. Heat a large pot over medium heat until hot, then pour in the oil, and tilt to coat the bottom. Add the leek and onion with a generous pinch sea salt, and cook for about 5 minutes, or until beginning to soften.

2. Add the tomato paste and red pepper flakes, and cook for about 2 minutes, or until everything is fragrant and beginning to caramelize.

3. Add the white wine, and simmer for about 2 minutes to cook off some of the alcohol.

4. Add the broth, bring to a simmer, and cook for 5 minutes.

5. Add the fresh salmon and heavy cream, and cook for 3 to 5 minutes, or until the salmon is just cooked through.

6. Add the smoked salmon, and stir briefly, allowing the flavors to come together for a minute or so.

7. Remove the pot from the heat, and stir in the parsley and dill.

INGREDIENT TIP: To wash the leek, slice it nearly in half lengthwise and rinse under cool running water. Dirt is easily trapped between the layers of the leek, so make sure to get into every crevice.

Ginger-Coconut Poached Salmon

DAIRY-FREE, GLUTEN-FREE, NUT-FREE, SOY-FREE

Serves 4 | **PREP TIME:** 5 minutes | **COOK TIME:** 10 minutes

This recipe has become my kids' favorite way to eat salmon—and mine, too. I love the way the creamy coconut milk gently poaches the salmon while infusing it with flavor. Ideally, choose wild salmon. Not only does it offer better nutrition, but it's also much better for the environment than farmed salmon, which is often produced unsustainably. Serve with Green Beans with Lemon and Mint (page 31) and Cauli Rice (page 29).

1 tablespoon coconut oil or
   canola oil

1 shallot, minced

1 tablespoon minced
   fresh ginger

1 teaspoon minced garlic

1 teaspoon sambal oelek or
   pinch red pepper flakes

1 (14-ounce) can coconut milk

1 pound salmon fillets

Juice of 1 lime

2 drops liquid stevia

1 scallion, green and white
   parts, thinly sliced

¼ cup coarsely chopped fresh
   cilantro

1. Heat a large skillet over medium heat until hot, then pour in the oil, and tilt to coat the bottom.
2. Add the shallot and ginger, and cook for about 2 minutes, or until fragrant.
3. Add the garlic, and cook for 30 seconds, or just until fragrant.
4. Stir in the sambal oelek and coconut milk, and bring to a simmer.
5. Add the salmon, and use a soup spoon to baste continuously with the coconut milk. Cook for about 5 minutes, or until the salmon can be flaked with a fork.
6. Stir in the lime juice and liquid stevia.
7. Garnish with the scallion and cilantro.

PER SERVING
Calories: 468;
Fat: 39g;
Saturated Fat: 26g;
Sodium: 123mg;
Total Carbohydrates: 8g;
Net Carbohydrates: 5g;
Fiber: 3g;
Sugar: 4g;
Protein: 25g

Hawaiian Ahi Poke

DAIRY-FREE, NUT-FREE

Serves 4 | **PREP TIME:** 10 minutes

Somewhere in between sushi and ceviche sits poke, a tasty raw fish dish that's served in a bowl. It's naturally low-carb and makes a delicious starter. To make it a complete meal, serve in a bowl with Cauli Rice (page 29) and alongside the Avocado-Citrus Salad (page 24). Choose sashimi-grade ahi tuna, which you can find at high-end supermarkets or fish markets in coastal areas.

1 pound sashimi-grade ahi tuna

1 large shallot, minced

2 scallions, green and white parts, thinly sliced

¼ cup low-sodium soy sauce

2 tablespoons mirin

1 tablespoon toasted sesame oil

1 teaspoon sambal oelek or pinch red pepper flakes

1 teaspoon sesame seeds

1 cucumber, peeled and thinly sliced

1. Cut the tuna into ½-inch cubes, and place in a bowl.
2. Add the shallot and scallions.
3. In another small bowl, whisk the soy sauce, mirin, sesame oil, and sambal oelek. Pour over the tuna, and toss gently to mix.
4. Just before serving, stir in the sesame seeds. Serve with the cucumber slices on top or on the side.

INGREDIENT TIP: Mirin is a Japanese sweet rice wine, and it's essential in teriyaki sauce, sushi rice, and this poke. In a pinch, you can also use rice-wine vinegar or a dry white wine. You may want to add a drop or two of liquid stevia to boost the sweetness.

PER SERVING
Calories: 172;
Fat: 5g;
Saturated Fat: 1g;
Sodium: 1016mg;
Total Carbohydrates: 8g;
Net Carbohydrates: 6g;
Fiber: 2g;
Sugar: 4g;
Protein: 25g

Niçoise Salad

DAIRY-FREE, GLUTEN-FREE, NUT-FREE, SOY-FREE

Serves 4 | **PREP TIME:** 10 minutes | **COOK TIME:** 20 minutes

This classic French salad has so many versions, and all claim authenticity. The basic concept is pretty simple though—boiled eggs, tuna, tomatoes, Niçoise olives, and fresh spring greens all dressed in a good-quality olive oil. Most versions include boiled potatoes, but they're hardly missed here. Instead, I tuck in a few other nonstarchy vegetables for a lower-carb version of the classic.

8 ounces green beans, trimmed

8 large eggs

8 ounces fresh tuna fillets

4 tablespoons extra-virgin olive oil, divided

Sea salt

Freshly ground black pepper

8 cups spring mix or baby salad greens

1 cup grape or cherry tomatoes, halved

1 cup marinated artichoke hearts, quartered and drained

½ cup Niçoise olives

Juice of ½ lemon

PER SERVING
Calories: 431;
Fat: 30g;
Saturated Fat: 6g;
Sodium: 643mg;
Total Carbohydrates: 15g;
Net Carbohydrates: 9g;
Fiber: 6g;
Sugar: 6g;
Protein: 28g

1. Bring a large pot of salted water to a steady boil, and fill a bowl with ice water.

2. Add the green beans, and cook for 3 minutes, or until bright green and crisp-tender. Use a slotted spoon to transfer to a colander, and rinse under cool running water briefly.

3. Return the water to a gentle boil, and add the eggs. Cook for 10 minutes, then transfer to the bowl of ice water.

4. Heat a large skillet over medium-high heat until hot.

5. Pat the tuna dry with paper towels, coat with 1 tablespoon of oil, and season generously with salt and pepper.

6. Put the tuna in the skillet, and sear for 2 minutes on each side for medium-rare. The fish will still be deep pink in the center.

7. Transfer the tuna to a cutting board. Cut into ½- to 1-inch-thick pieces.

8. Once the eggs are cool, peel under cool running water, then slice in half.

9. To serve, divide the salad greens, eggs, tuna, tomatoes, artichoke hearts, olives, and green beans among 4 serving dishes. Drizzle with the remaining 3 tablespoons of oil and the lemon juice.

Sugar Snap Pea Stir-Fry with Seared Tuna

DAIRY-FREE, NUT-FREE

Serves 4 | **PREP TIME:** 10 minutes | **COOK TIME:** 10 minutes

Plenty of dinner delivery services will send you a box of ingredients and a recipe with the promise that you'll have dinner on the table in less than 30 minutes. Why not do that for yourself? This recipe is easy to prep ahead of time and then toss in a pan for a satisfying meal at a moment's notice. Bonus: You'll skip the packaging and the high price tag.

4 (6-ounce) tuna steaks

2 tablespoons canola oil, divided

Sea salt

Freshly ground black pepper

1 tablespoon toasted sesame oil

1 pound sugar snap peas, trimmed

1 bunch radishes, thinly sliced

1 teaspoon minced fresh ginger

¼ cup soy sauce

2 tablespoons freshly squeezed lime juice

2 or 3 drops liquid stevia

PER SERVING
Calories: 298;
Fat: 11g;
Saturated Fat: 1g;
Sodium: 994mg;
Total Carbohydrates: 13g;
Net Carbohydrates: 9g;
Fiber: 4g;
Sugar: 6g;
Protein: 39g

1. Heat a large skillet over medium-high heat until hot.

2. Pat the tuna dry with paper towels, and coat with 1 tablespoon of canola oil. Season generously with salt and pepper.

3. Put the tuna in the skillet, and sear for about 2 minutes on each side for medium-rare. It should still be deep pink in the center. Set aside on a cutting board and tent with foil.

4. Add the remaining 1 tablespoon of canola oil and the sesame oil to the skillet.

5. Add the snap peas, and stir-fry for 2 minutes, or until bright green.

6. Add the radishes and ginger, and sauté for 1 minute, or just until heated through and fragrant.

7. Add the soy sauce, lime juice, and liquid stevia, and toss gently to coat the vegetables in the mixture.

8. To serve, cut the tuna into ½- to 1-inch-thick slices. Serve with the sautéed vegetables on the side.

INGREDIENT TIP: To trim the snap peas, use a paring knife to cut off the stem end. Use the knife and your thumb to gently peel the string from the side of each pod.

Miso-Glazed Cod with Baby Bok Choy

DAIRY-FREE, NUT-FREE

Serves 4 | **PREP TIME:** 5 minutes | **COOK TIME:** 10 minutes

If you haven't tried miso yet, you're in for a surprise. It's fermented soybean paste that is salty, funky, and barely sweet. It lends a delicious quality to nearly everything it touches. Start with white miso paste for a mild flavor. Pretty soon, you'll find yourself whisking it into everything from salads to ice cream. (Yes, for real!) You can find it refrigerated in the grocery store, often next to the tofu, tempeh, and specialty vegan foods.

2 tablespoons toasted sesame oil, divided

2 tablespoons white miso

2 tablespoons low-sodium soy sauce, divided

2 tablespoons freshly squeezed lime juice

1 tablespoon minced fresh ginger

2 or 3 drops liquid stevia

4 (6-ounce) cod fillets

2 pounds baby bok choy, halved lengthwise

1 teaspoon minced garlic

Pinch red pepper flakes

PER SERVING
Calories: 253;
Fat: 9g;
Saturated Fat: 1g;
Sodium: 1098mg;
Total Carbohydrates: 10g;
Net Carbohydrates: 7g;
Fiber: 3g;
Sugar: 4g;
Protein: 35g

1. Preheat the oven to 325°F.
2. In a small bowl, combine 1 tablespoon of sesame oil, the miso, 1 tablespoon of soy sauce, the lime juice, ginger, and liquid stevia.
3. Coat the cod fillets in the mixture, and put them in a baking dish.
4. Transfer the baking dish to the oven, and bake for 10 to 12 minutes, or until the fish flakes easily with a fork.
5. Meanwhile, heat a large skillet over medium-high heat until hot, then pour in the remaining 1 tablespoon of oil, and tilt to coat the bottom.
6. Place the bok choy in the skillet, cut-side down. It will pop and splatter, so stand back a bit at first. You may also need to lower the heat slightly. Sear the bok choy until well browned, about 4 minutes.
7. Flip, and cook for 2 minutes, or until it is fork-tender.
8. Add the garlic and red pepper flakes, then remove from the heat.
9. Drizzle with the remaining 1 tablespoon of soy sauce, and toss gently to disburse the garlic, red pepper flakes, and soy sauce.
10. Serve the cod with the bok choy on the side.

Tomato-Basil Poached Cod

DAIRY-FREE, GLUTEN-FREE, NUT-FREE, SOY-FREE

Serves 4 | **PREP TIME:** 5 minutes | **COOK TIME:** 15 minutes

Sweet tomatoes, fragrant basil, and pungent garlic infuse this mild fish with flavor. Serve with Mediterranean Zucchini Hummus (page 20), assorted raw vegetables, and the rest of the bottle of white wine for a refreshing summer supper.

¼ cup extra-virgin olive oil

1 tablespoon minced garlic

1 pound grape
   tomatoes, halved

¼ cup dry white wine

Zest and juice of 1 lemon

1 cup minced fresh basil

4 (6-ounce) cod fillets

Sea salt

Freshly ground black pepper

PER SERVING
Calories: 280;
Fat: 14g;
Saturated Fat: 2g;
Sodium: 170mg;
Total Carbohydrates: 6g;
Net Carbohydrates: 4g;
Fiber: 2g;
Sugar: 3g;
Protein: 31g

1. Heat a large skillet over medium heat until hot, then pour in the oil, and tilt to coat the bottom.
2. Add the garlic, and cook for about 30 seconds, or just until fragrant.
3. Add the tomatoes, and cook for 5 minutes, or until the tomatoes soften.
4. Increase the heat to medium-high, and add the white wine. Simmer for 2 minutes to cook off some of the alcohol.
5. Stir in the lemon zest and juice and basil.
6. Season the cod fillets with salt and pepper, and nestle them into the tomato mixture. Cook for about 3 minutes.
7. Flip, and cook for 3 minutes, or until the cod flakes easily with a fork.

INGREDIENT TIP: I like to buy the heirloom grape and cherry tomatoes from Trader Joe's because they come in a beautiful medley of yellows, oranges, and reds.

Basil Butter Grilled Shrimp

GLUTEN-FREE, NUT-FREE, SOY-FREE

Serves 4 | **PREP TIME:** 10 minutes | **COOK TIME:** 5 minutes

Compound butters are a staple in the low-carb kitchen, and they're super easy to make. Just mash your favorite combination of herbs and spices into a small dish of butter, shape it into a log, wrap in plastic wrap, and refrigerate. Then, whenever you need a boost of flavor, slice off a piece or two. It's perfect atop seared steak, steamed vegetables, or, as in this recipe, softened and stuffed into shrimp just before they hit the grill. The butter bastes them from inside the shells, locking in all of those tasty flavors.

8 tablespoons (1 stick) butter, softened

¼ cup minced basil

1 teaspoon minced garlic

Zest of 1 lime

2 pounds EZ-peel large or extra-large shrimp

Juice of 1 lime

PER SERVING
Calories: 431;
Fat: 25g;
Saturated Fat: 15g;
Sodium: 671mg;
Total Carbohydrates: 1g;
Net Carbohydrates: 1g;
Fiber: 0g;
Sugar: 0g;
Protein: 48g

1. Preheat a gas grill to medium, or fire up a charcoal grill. (If you do not have an outdoor grill, cook the shrimp in a large cast-iron skillet over medium heat.)

2. In a small bowl, combine the butter, basil, garlic, and lime zest.

3. Carefully tuck the compound butter in between the shells and flesh of the shrimp, then thread them onto bamboo skewers. (With EZ-peel shrimp, the shells are already sliced down the back, so you can open them up a bit and add the compound butter. Otherwise, use a small, sharp knife to slit each shell open along the back. Devein.)

4. Put the shrimp on the grill, and cook for about 2 minutes on each side, or until just cooked through.

5. To serve, transfer the skewers to a platter, and shower with lime juice.

VARIATION TIP: Change things up with a smoky chipotle compound butter. Replace the basil with 1 tablespoon smoked paprika and 1 teaspoon ground chipotle pepper.

Shrimp Scampi

GLUTEN-FREE, NUT-FREE, SOY-FREE

Serves 4 | **PREP TIME:** 10 minutes | **COOK TIME:** 5 to 10 minutes

Shrimp scampi is a staple at seafood restaurants because the flavors are familiar and delicious. But most restaurants go heavy on the pasta and light on the shrimp. This low-carb version shows you just how easy it is to capture all of those delicious flavors while kicking carbs to the curb. Instead of a heaping bowl of pasta, serve it atop a bowl of Cauli Rice (page 29).

2 tablespoons extra-virgin
  olive oil

2 tablespoons butter

1 tablespoon minced garlic

2 shallots, minced

½ cup dry white wine

1½ pounds extra-large
  shrimp, peeled

Sea salt

Freshly ground black pepper

Juice of ½ lemon

¼ cup minced fresh
  flat-leaf parsley

1. Heat a large skillet over medium heat until hot, then pour in the oil, and melt the butter. Tilt to coat the bottom.
2. Add the garlic and shallots, and cook for about 3 minutes, or until they begin to soften.
3. Add the wine, and cook for about 2 minutes to cook off some of the alcohol.
4. Add the shrimp, and sauté for 2 to 3 minutes, stirring and flipping to cook on all sides, or until just cooked through.
5. Season with salt and pepper, sprinkle with lemon juice, and garnish with the parsley.

INGREDIENT TIP: The Monterey Bay Aquarium Seafood Watch recommends choosing freshwater prawns grown in ponds in the Americas for the least environmental impact and the healthiest choice.

PER SERVING
Calories: 312;
Fat: 15g;
Saturated Fat: 5g;
Sodium: 485mg;
Total Carbohydrates: 3g;
Net Carbohydrates: 3g;
Fiber: 0g;
Sugar: 0g;
Protein: 36g

Green Curry Shrimp and Vegetables

DAIRY-FREE, GLUTEN-FREE, NUT-FREE, SOY-FREE

Serves 4 | **PREP TIME:** 10 minutes | **COOK TIME:** 15 minutes

Green curry paste is almost magical in its ability to imbue foods with flavor. It can transform basic veggies into a savory curry straight from Thailand. You can find green curry paste in the Asian foods section of your local grocery store, where you'll also be able to pick up a couple of cans of coconut milk and a bottle of fish sauce.

1 tablespoon coconut oil

1 small red onion, halved and sliced

1 eggplant, cut into 1-inch dice

1 head broccoli, cut into florets

3 tablespoons green curry paste

1 red bell pepper, cut into 2-inch-thick strips

½ pound green beans, trimmed and cut into 2-inch pieces

2 (14-ounce) cans coconut milk

2 tablespoons fish sauce

1 pound large shrimp, peeled

¼ cup coarsely chopped fresh cilantro

2 tablespoons freshly squeezed lime juice

2 or 3 drops liquid stevia

1. Heat a large pot over medium-high heat until hot, then pour in the oil, and tilt to coat the bottom.

2. Add the onion, and cook for 2 to 3 minutes, or until beginning to soften.

3. Add the eggplant and broccoli, and cook for 2 to 3 minutes, or until beginning to soften.

4. Add the curry paste and cook for about 1 minute, or until fragrant.

5. Add the bell pepper, green beans, coconut milk, and fish sauce. Bring to a simmer and cook for 5 minutes, or until the vegetables are crisp-tender.

6. Add the shrimp, cover the pot, and cook for 2 to 3 minutes, or until the shrimp are just cooked through. Do not overcook.

7. Remove from the heat, and stir in the cilantro, lime juice, and stevia.

PER SERVING
Calories: 704;
Fat: 55g;
Saturated Fat: 46g;
Sodium: 1905mg;
Total Carbohydrates: 34g;
Net Carbohydrates: 20g;
Fiber: 14g;
Sugar: 15g;
Protein: 30g

COOKING TIP: Want to know when your shrimp is done? Just look at the way it curves. When it is opaque and forms a gentle C shape, it's done. If it's bordering on the letter O, it's overcooked.

Mussels Veracruz

DAIRY-FREE, GLUTEN-FREE, NUT-FREE, SOY-FREE

Serves 4 | **PREP TIME:** 10 minutes | **COOK TIME:** 15 to 20 minutes

The signature dish of Veracruz, Mexico, fish Veracruz takes whatever seafood is fresh and brings it to life on the plate with briny capers, savory olives, chiles, and plenty of onions and garlic. This version uses fresh mussels, but choose whatever seafood looks best at your fish market. Actually, the frozen section is a surprisingly good place for sourcing sustainable seafood because it's quick-frozen—within hours of being caught. Serve with Parmesan Crisps (page 18) and Cauli Rice (page 29).

2 tablespoons extra-virgin olive oil

1 onion, diced

1 tablespoon minced garlic

1 serrano chile, minced

1 (15-ounce) can whole plum tomatoes, hand crushed

½ cup coarsely chopped pitted green olives

¼ cup drained capers

3 fresh oregano sprigs, stemmed and minced

2 fresh marjoram sprigs, stemmed and minced

2 bay leaves

2 pounds fresh mussels, scrubbed and debearded

½ cup dry white wine

PER SERVING
Calories: 349;
Fat: 18g;
Saturated Fat: 3g;
Sodium: 1975mg;
Total Carbohydrates: 16g;
Net Carbohydrates: 13g;
Fiber: 3g;
Sugar: 4g;
Protein: 21g

1. Heat a large skillet over medium heat until hot, then pour in the oil, and tilt to coat the bottom.

2. Add the onion, garlic, and chile, and cook for 5 minutes, or until beginning to soften.

3. Add the tomatoes, olives, capers, oregano, marjoram, and bay leaves, and cook for about 2 minutes, or until fragrant.

4. Add the mussels, then add the white wine. Cover with a tight-fitting lid and simmer for 8 to 10 minutes. All of the mussels should have opened by then. Any that don't open after 10 minutes should be discarded.

INGREDIENT TIP: If you're new to cooking mussels, here's a primer on how to handle them. Buy them the same day you'll serve them, and store them in a breathable container (such as a net bag) in the refrigerator. Just before cooking, scrub them with a vegetable brush under cool running water and remove the tough, stringy "beards" attached to them. Discard any with broken (not barely chipped) shells.

Italian Sausage and Mussels

DAIRY-FREE, GLUTEN-FREE, NUT-FREE, SOY-FREE

Serves 4 | **PREP TIME:** 5 minutes | **COOK TIME:** 25 minutes

This indulgent dish is somewhere in between a stew and a sauce. I first enjoyed it at an Italian restaurant in Marin County, California, where epic views of the valley below and the city in the distance competed with the exceptional food for my attention. Hot Italian sausage, dry red wine, and plenty of fresh basil bring layers of complexity to steamed mussels. It's delicious served over Celery Root Purée (page 27) with a green salad on the side.

8 ounces hot Italian sausage, casings removed, crumbled

1 medium onion, finely diced

1 tablespoon minced garlic

1 cup dry red wine

2 tablespoons tomato paste

2 cups chicken stock

1½ pounds fresh mussels, scrubbed and debearded

1 cup coarsely chopped fresh basil

PER SERVING
Calories: 330;
Fat: 14g;
Saturated Fat: 4g;
Sodium: 1092mg;
Total Carbohydrates: 12g;
Net Carbohydrates: 10g;
Fiber: 2g;
Sugar: 3g;
Protein: 26g

1. Heat a large skillet over medium-high heat until hot.
2. Put the sausage in the skillet, and cook for 5 to 7 minutes, or until just cooked through. Transfer to a small bowl.
3. Add the onion to the skillet, and cook for 5 minutes, or until beginning to soften.
4. Add the garlic, and cook for 30 seconds, or just until fragrant.
5. Add the red wine, scraping up the browned bits from the bottom.
6. Stir in the tomato paste and chicken stock, and bring to a simmer.
7. Add the mussels, cover with a tight-fitting lid, and steam for 8 to 10 minutes. All of the mussels should have opened by then. Any that don't open after 10 minutes should be discarded.
8. Stir in the basil and sausage and any accumulated juices.

Cioppino

DAIRY-FREE, GLUTEN-FREE, NUT-FREE, SOY-FREE

Serves 4 | **PREP TIME:** 10 minutes | **COOK TIME:** 20 minutes

This fragrant seafood stew originated in San Francisco among Italian immigrants who worked the fishing boats. It was typically made with whatever the day's fresh catch was, along with plenty of onions, garlic, tomatoes, and wine. I've experimented a lot with this stew over the years and have finally found a version that lives up to its rich history.

3 tablespoons olive oil

1 onion, diced

6 garlic cloves, minced

½ cup coarsely chopped plum tomatoes

¼ teaspoon red pepper flakes

2 tablespoons tomato paste

½ cup dry white wine

8 cups vegetable broth or seafood stock

1½ pounds clams or mussels, scrubbed and debearded

1 pound firm white fish fillets, cut into 2-inch pieces

½ pound peeled large shrimp

Sea salt

Freshly ground black pepper

2 scallions, green and white parts, thinly sliced

½ bunch fresh flat-leaf parsley, minced

Juice of ½ lemon

1. Heat a large pot over medium-high heat until hot, then pour in the oil, and tilt to coat the bottom.
2. Add the onion, and cook for about 5 minutes, or until beginning to soften.
3. Add the garlic, tomatoes, and red pepper flakes, and cook for 2 minutes, or until fragrant.
4. Add the tomato paste, and cook for 2 minutes, or until it begins to caramelize.
5. Add the white wine and broth, and bring to a simmer.
6. Add the clams or mussels, cover with a tight-fitting lid, and cook for 5 minutes.
7. Add the fish, replace the lid, and cook for 2 minutes.
8. Stir in the shrimp, replace the lid, and cook for 3 minutes. (Total cooking time for all the seafood is 10 minutes.) All of the mussels should have opened by then. Any that don't open after 10 minutes should be discarded. Season with salt and pepper.
9. Stir in the scallions, parsley, and a generous squeeze of lemon juice just before serving.

PER SERVING
Calories: 479;
Fat: 18g;
Saturated Fat: 3g;
Sodium: 1043mg;
Total Carbohydrates: 17g;
Net Carbohydrates: 13g;
Fiber: 4g;
Sugar: 5g;
Protein: 57g

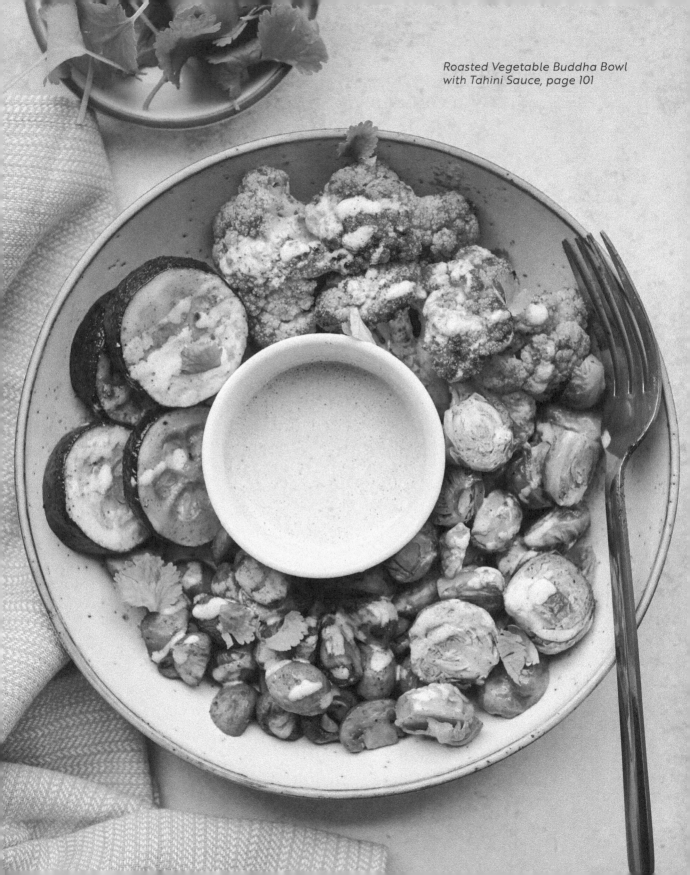

*Roasted Vegetable Buddha Bowl
with Tahini Sauce, page 101*

6

vegetarian

Zucchini Noodles with Pepitas and Avocado

DAIRY-FREE, GLUTEN-FREE, SOY-FREE, VEGAN

Serves 4 | **PREP TIME:** 10 minutes

Spicy chipotle peppers and lime juice are blended into a creamy, cashew-based dressing in this tangy raw, vegan noodle bowl. It has plenty of healthy fats from the nuts and avocado, which help your body absorb the nutrients in the other vegetables. Edamame and pepitas provide a little extra dose of protein, so this meal will stay with you for hours. You can buy edamame (whole soybeans) in their pods or shelled, most likely in the freezer section of the supermarket. You'll find canned chipotle peppers in adobo sauce in the international foods aisle.

2 medium zucchini

½ cup raw unsalted cashews, soaked in fresh water

½ cup water

1 to 2 teaspoons minced chipotle peppers in adobo sauce

Juice of 1 lime

½ teaspoon sea salt

1 large avocado, pitted, peeled, and diced

1 large ripe tomato, diced

1 red bell pepper, thinly sliced

1 cup shelled edamame

½ cup coarsely chopped fresh cilantro

¼ cup pepitas

1. Run the zucchini through a spiralizer or use a vegetable peeler to slice it into thin ribbons.

2. Put the cashews, water, chipotles, lime juice, and salt in a blender, and purée until very smooth, adding more water and scraping down the sides as needed.

3. Pour this mixture over the zucchini, and toss gently to coat. Divide among 4 serving dishes.

4. Top each noodle bowl with some avocado, tomato, bell pepper, edamame, cilantro, and pepitas.

COOKING TIP: When using cashews or other nuts to make a creamy sauce, soak them in fresh water for 4 to 8 hours to soften and make them easier to blend. Rinse and drain before using.

PER SERVING
Calories: 252;
Fat: 19g;
Saturated Fat: 3g;
Sodium: 260mg;
Total Carbohydrates: 16g;
Net Carbohydrates: 9g;
Fiber: 7g;
Sugar: 3g;
Protein: 8g

Raw Taco Salad with Pico de Gallo

DAIRY-FREE, GLUTEN-FREE, SOY-FREE, VEGAN

Serves 4 | **PREP TIME:** 10 minutes

This was one of the first raw, vegan meals I ever tried, and I was instantly hooked. This dish makes a perfect light summer dinner and is a great option for advance meal prepping. Bonus: Because everything is raw, you get all of the nutritional benefits of plants—antioxidants, phytonutrients, vitamins, minerals, and plenty of fiber.

For the pico de gallo

4 large ripe tomatoes, diced
1 garlic clove, minced
1 jalapeño pepper, seeded
   and minced
Juice of 1 lime
½ cup chopped fresh cilantro
¼ cup minced red onion
Sea salt

For the tacos

½ cup raw unsalted walnuts
½ cup raw unsalted pecans
1 teaspoon ground cumin
½ teaspoon ground coriander
1 teaspoon sea salt
2 tablespoons olive oil
8 cups shredded lettuce

PER SERVING
Calories: 562;
Fat: 39g;
Saturated Fat: 4g;
Sodium: 500mg;
Total Carbohydrates: 27g;
Net Carbohydrates: 17g;
Fiber: 10g;
Sugar: 9g;
Protein: 11g

TO MAKE THE PICO DE GALLO

In a large mixing bowl, combine the tomatoes, garlic, jalapeño pepper, lime juice, cilantro, and onion. Season with salt.

TO MAKE THE TACOS

1. To make the taco nut meat, put the walnuts, pecans, cumin, coriander, and salt in a food processor, and pulse until coarsely ground.
2. With the motor still running, drizzle in the oil.
3. To serve, divide the lettuce among 4 serving bowls. Top with the taco nut meat and pico de gallo. Add some guacamole (page 64), if desired, and serve immediately.

LEFTOVERS: Store each of the components of this recipe in separate containers in the refrigerator for up to two days.

Vegan Cobb Salad with Shiitake Bacon

DAIRY-FREE, GLUTEN-FREE, SOY-FREE, VEGAN

Serves 4 | **PREP TIME:** 5 minutes | **COOK TIME:** 25 minutes

When I approached this recipe, I had two options: Keep all of the traditional elements of Cobb salad except the bacon, or create a completely plant-based version of everything. I'm betting that you could easily figure out the former option, so I went with this vegan version. The shiitake bacon takes a bit of prep, so it's great to make on the weekend and serve all week long.

For the shiitake bacon

2 tablespoons canola oil

1 or 2 drops liquid stevia

¼ teaspoon liquid smoke (optional)

¼ teaspoon sea salt

8 ounces shiitake mushrooms, sliced

TO MAKE THE SHIITAKE BACON

1. Preheat the oven to 375°F. Line a rimmed baking sheet with parchment paper.

2. In a large mixing bowl, whisk the canola oil, liquid stevia, liquid smoke (if using), and salt.

3. Add the mushrooms, and toss gently to mix.

4. Spread the mushrooms onto the baking sheet, transfer to the oven, and bake for 20 to 25 minutes, flipping occasionally, or until they are gently browned and beginning to dry out. Be careful not to burn.

For the salad

½ cup extra-virgin olive oil

¼ cup red-wine vinegar

¼ teaspoon Dijon mustard

Sea salt

Freshly ground
    black pepper

8 cups shredded
    romaine lettuce

1 cup grape
    tomatoes, halved

2 large avocados, pitted,
    peeled, and diced

6 to 8 ounces vegan soft
    nut cheese, such as
    Treeline or Miyoko's
    Creamery

PER SERVING

Calories: 180;
Fat: 66g;
Saturated Fat: 9g;
Sodium: 462mg;
Total Carbohydrates: 28g;
Net Carbohydrates: 17g;
Fiber: 11g;
Sugar: 5g;
Protein: 12g

TO MAKE THE SALAD

1. While the mushrooms are cooking, in a small jar, to make the dressing, whisk together the olive oil, vinegar, and mustard. Season with salt and pepper.

2. Put the lettuce and tomatoes in a large bowl, and drizzle with the dressing. Toss gently to coat.

3. Divide the salad among 4 serving plates. Top with the avocados, a few bite-size pieces of the vegan cheese, and the shiitake bacon.

VARIATION TIP: For a nut-free version, replace the nut cheese with shredded vegan cheese, such as Follow Your Heart Gourmet Shreds, or if you eat dairy, try traditional Gorgonzola cheese.

Thai Peanut Tempeh Salad

DAIRY-FREE, VEGAN

Serves 4 | **PREP TIME:** 5 minutes | **COOK TIME:** 15 minutes

Is there anything more addictive than Thai peanut sauce? It offers the perfect balance of salty, sweet, and sour. There's only one little problem: Most are filled with sugar—as much as 6 grams per serving. Save the cash and the carbs, and make your own. It's a lot easier than you think.

1 (1-inch) piece fresh
 ginger, peeled

1 garlic clove

½ cup creamy natural
 peanut butter

¼ cup warm water

2 tablespoons soy sauce

2 tablespoons lime juice

1 teaspoon sambal oelek or
 pinch red pepper flakes

1 or 2 drops liquid stevia

1 (8-ounce) block tempeh

1 tablespoon canola oil

4 cups shredded lettuce

2 cups shredded red cabbage

2 carrots, spiralized or cut
 into ribbons

1 cup hand-torn fresh herbs,
 such as basil and mint

½ cup coarsely chopped
 roasted unsalted peanuts

1 lime, cut into wedges

PER SERVING
Calories: 433;
Fat: 32g;
Saturated Fat: 6g;
Sodium: 452mg;
Total Carbohydrates: 20g;
Net Carbohydrates: 14g;
Fiber: 6g;
Sugar: 6g;
Protein: 25g

1. Preheat the oven to 350°F. Line a rimmed baking sheet with parchment paper.

2. To make the peanut sauce, put the ginger, garlic, peanut butter, water, soy sauce, lime juice, sambal oelek, and liquid stevia in a blender, and purée until smooth, adding more water and scraping down the sides as needed.

3. Cut the tempeh in half, then turn each slice on its side, and cut in half. Cut these blocks into 2-inch pieces.

4. Put the tempeh in a shallow dish. Pour half the peanut sauce and all of the canola oil over the tempeh, and turn to coat. Transfer to a rimmed baking sheet.

5. Transfer the baking sheet to the oven, and roast for 12 minutes, or until sticky and beginning to brown.

6. Put the lettuce, cabbage, carrots, and herbs in a large serving bowl or 4 individual bowls. Top with the roasted tempeh. Garnish with the chopped peanuts and lime wedges.

INGREDIENT TIP: Tempeh is fermented soybeans pressed into a cake. It's similar to tofu, but is less processed. You can find it at some supermarkets and most health food stores, with the refrigerated foods.

Shawarma-Spiced Tempeh with Cucumber

GLUTEN-FREE, NUT-FREE, VEGETARIAN

Serves 4 | **PREP TIME:** 10 minutes | **COOK TIME:** 20 minutes

If you think shawarma and tempeh don't belong in the same sentence, let alone the same recipe, prepare to be amazed. Traditionally, shawarma is made from thin pieces of marinated lamb or another meat, stacked onto a skewer and then cooked on a spit. Making it plant-based is simply a matter of mixing up those spices and applying them to tempeh. It works best if you can let the tempeh sit in the spice mixture overnight, but whatever time you have is fine.

3 tablespoons extra-virgin olive oil

2 teaspoons ground coriander

2 teaspoons smoked paprika

1 teaspoon ground cumin

1 teaspoon sea salt

¼ teaspoon cayenne pepper

¼ teaspoon ground cinnamon

2 (8-ounce) blocks tempeh

1 cucumber, diced

1 large ripe tomato, diced

½ red onion, thinly sliced

1 tablespoon red-wine vinegar

1 teaspoon minced fresh dill

1 cup whole-milk plain yogurt

PER SERVING
Calories: 378;
Fat: 25g;
Saturated Fat: 5g;
Sodium: 513mg;
Total Carbohydrates: 20g;
Net Carbohydrates: 17g;
Fiber: 3g;
Sugar: 6g;
Protein: 25g

1. Preheat the oven to 375°F.
2. In a wide shallow baking dish, combine the oil, coriander, paprika, cumin, salt, cayenne pepper, and cinnamon.
3. Carefully cut the tempeh in half horizontally, then cut each piece into 4 or 5 triangles.
4. Transfer to the baking dish, and turn very gently to coat.
5. Transfer the baking dish to the oven, and roast for 15 minutes, or until beginning to brown.
6. Flip, then roast for 5 minutes, being careful not to burn.
7. Meanwhile, in a large mixing bowl, combine the cucumber, tomato, onion, vinegar, and dill.
8. To serve, divide the tempeh among 4 serving dishes. Serve the cucumber salad and spoonfuls of yogurt on the side.

VARIATION TIP: To make this recipe vegan, swap out the yogurt for ¼ cup good-quality tahini whisked together with 2 tablespoons of lemon juice and a pinch sea salt.

Smoky Cauliflower Zucchini Hash

GLUTEN-FREE, NUT-FREE, SOY-FREE, VEGETARIAN

Serves 4 | **PREP TIME:** 10 minutes | **COOK TIME:** 20 minutes

This oven-roasted dinnertime hash is bursting with flavor. But unlike typical hashes that rely on potatoes, this one is built on crunchy cauliflower, succulent zucchini, and flavorful mushrooms. While you can certainly go for fried eggs, I opt for a healthier preparation method here— poaching. Ignore whatever you've heard about poaching eggs being difficult. It's actually quite simple.

1 head cauliflower, cut into
   1-inch pieces

2 medium zucchini, cut into
   1-inch pieces

1 pint cremini or button
   mushrooms

1 onion, halved and sliced

2 tablespoons extra-virgin
   olive oil

1 tablespoon smoked paprika

2 teaspoons minced
   fresh thyme

½ teaspoon sea salt

¼ teaspoon apple cider vinegar
   or white vinegar

4 large eggs

About 1 ounce Parmesan
   cheese, shaved

PER SERVING
Calories: 203;
Fat: 14g;
Saturated Fat: 4g;
Sodium: 365mg;
Total Carbohydrates: 12g;
Net Carbohydrates: 7g;
Fiber: 5g;
Sugar: 6g;
Protein: 12g

1. Preheat the oven to 400°F. Line a rimmed baking sheet with parchment paper.

2. In a large mixing bowl, combine the cauliflower, zucchini, mushrooms, onion, oil, paprika, thyme, and salt, then toss gently to coat. Spread the mixture onto the baking sheet.

3. Transfer the baking sheet to the oven, and roast for 20 minutes, or until the vegetables are crisp-tender and beginning to brown.

4. Meanwhile, fill a medium saucepan with 2 inches of water, then add the vinegar, and heat over medium heat.

5. Crack the eggs into individual bowls. Once the water has come to a gentle simmer, carefully slide each egg out of its bowl and into the water. Make sure the water does not reach a vigorous boil. Set a timer for 2 to 3 minutes, depending on how you like your eggs done.

6. To serve, divide the roasted vegetables among 4 serving dishes. Remove each egg from the pan with a slotted spoon. Top each veggie dish with a poached egg and a few shavings of Parmesan.

COOKING TIP: To shave Parmesan cheese, simply scrape some off the wedge with a vegetable peeler.

Cauliflower Steaks with Romesco and Crumbled Feta

GLUTEN-FREE, SOY-FREE, VEGETARIAN

Serves 4 | **PREP TIME:** 10 minutes | **COOK TIME:** 20 minutes

Have you ever noticed how a good sauce can transform the most mundane ingredients into an extraordinary meal? Romesco is one such sauce, and it packs a flavor punch from roasted red peppers, hazelnuts, and red-wine vinegar. You can roast both pans of veggies at the same time, and then make the sauce while the cauliflower finishes cooking. This meal is loaded with flavor but overall pretty light on calories.

2 red bell peppers, seeded and quartered

2 large ripe tomatoes, seeded and quartered

3 garlic cloves, unpeeled

4 tablespoons extra-virgin olive oil, divided

Sea salt

1 large cauliflower, cut vertically into 4 thick slices

¼ cup coarsely chopped roasted hazelnuts

¼ cup red-wine vinegar

2 tablespoons fresh flat-leaf parsley, plus more

4 ounces crumbled feta cheese

PER SERVING
Calories: 316;
Fat: 25g;
Saturated Fat: 7g;
Sodium: 445mg;
Total Carbohydrates: 18g;
Net Carbohydrates: 11g;
Fiber: 7g;
Sugar: 9g;
Protein: 10g

1. Preheat the oven to 425°F.

2. Spread the bell peppers, tomatoes, and garlic onto a rimmed baking sheet. Drizzle with 2 tablespoons of oil, and toss to coat. Season with salt.

3. Transfer the baking sheet to the oven, and roast for 15 minutes, flipping the ingredients once to brown on both sides.

4. Put the cauliflower pieces on another rimmed baking sheet, and drizzle with the remaining 2 tablespoons of oil. Season with salt. Cover the pan tightly with foil.

5. Transfer the baking sheet to the oven, and roast for 10 minutes.

6. Uncover, flip, and return to the oven. Roast for another 10 minutes, or until barely charred.

7. To make the romesco sauce, carefully peel the roasted garlic, and transfer to a blender, along with the bell peppers, tomatoes, hazelnuts, red-wine vinegar, and parsley. Blend until mostly smooth, scraping down the sides as needed. Season with salt.

8. To serve, spread some of the romesco sauce on each serving plate, and top with the cauliflower steaks. Garnish with the feta and some parsley.

Roasted Squash and Goat Cheese Crustless Quiche

GLUTEN-FREE, NUT-FREE, SOY-FREE, VEGETARIAN

Serves 4 | **PREP TIME:** 5 minutes | **COOK TIME:** 25 minutes

Initially I had a traditional quiche in a fluted tart pan in mind for this recipe, but time constraints got in the way, and I wanted a one-dish meal that you didn't need to make a pastry crust for. Even a low-carb almond flour crust just sounded too fussy. I landed on this crustless quiche, which offers some surprising flavors from tangy goat cheese and sweet roasted butternut squash.

1 small butternut squash, peeled, seeded, and cut into 1-inch cubes

1 small onion, cut into 1-inch slices

2 tablespoons extra-virgin olive oil

Sea salt

1 (8-ounce) log goat cheese, crumbled

½ cup whole milk

6 large eggs

2 tablespoons minced fresh flat-leaf parsley

1. Preheat the oven to 425°F.
2. Put the butternut squash and onion in an 8-by-8-inch baking dish, then drizzle with the oil, and toss gently to coat. Season with salt.
3. Transfer the baking dish to the oven, and roast for 15 minutes, or until the butternut squash is nearly tender and beginning to brown.
4. Sprinkle the goat cheese over the roasted squash.
5. In a medium bowl, whisk the milk and eggs, and season with salt.
6. Pour this mixture over the goat cheese and squash, and top with the parsley.
7. Return the baking dish to the oven, and cook for 10 minutes, or until the quiche is set.

PER SERVING
Calories: 419;
Fat: 25g;
Saturated Fat: 11g;
Sodium: 382mg;
Total Carbohydrates: 24g;
Net Carbohydrates: 19g;
Fiber: 5g;
Sugar: 7g;
Protein: 17g

VARIATION TIP: Not a fan of goat cheese? Swap it for another soft cheese. Even cream cheese will work fine.

Roasted Vegetable Buddha Bowl with Tahini Sauce

DAIRY-FREE, GLUTEN-FREE, NUT-FREE, SOY-FREE, VEGAN

Serves 4 | **PREP TIME:** 10 minutes | **COOK TIME:** 20 minutes

This 100-percent plant-based bowl is the antidote to the heavy meals that often dominate low-carb cooking. With Brussels sprouts, paprika-spiced cauliflower, earthy mushrooms, and roasted zucchini, it's also a feast for the eyes. The tahini sauce is adapted from a recipe in one of my favorite vegan cookbooks, The Plantpower Way *by Rich Roll. His book illustrates that even vegan cooking can be centered primarily on fresh, nonstarchy vegetables—it's not all pasta and grains! The tahini sauce is so addictive, you'll want to pour it over everything.*

For the vegetables

1 head cauliflower, cored and cut into florets
4 tablespoons extra-virgin olive oil, divided
1 tablespoon smoked paprika
Sea salt
1 medium zucchini, cut into 1-inch pieces
8 ounces Brussels sprouts, halved
1 pint cremini or button mushrooms, trimmed and halved
Freshly ground black pepper

TO MAKE THE VEGETABLES

1. Preheat the oven to 400°F. Line a rimmed baking sheet with parchment paper.
2. In a large bowl, toss the cauliflower with 1 tablespoon of oil and the smoked paprika. Season with salt. Spread onto one end of the baking sheet.
3. In the same bowl, toss the zucchini with 1 tablespoon of oil. Season with salt. Spread onto the baking sheet next to the cauliflower.
4. In the same bowl, toss the Brussels sprouts with 1 tablespoon of oil. Season with salt. Spread onto the baking sheet next to the zucchini.
5. In the same bowl, toss the mushrooms with the remaining 1 tablespoon of oil. Season with salt. Spread onto the baking sheet next to the Brussels sprouts.
6. Roast for 20 minutes, or until the vegetables are gently browned and tender but not burned.

continued on next page...

For the tahini sauce

1 cup water

½ cup minced fresh cilantro

⅓ cup tahini

2 tablespoons freshly squeezed
    lemon juice

1 tablespoon apple
    cider vinegar

1 teaspoon garlic powder

½ teaspoon sea salt

1 or 2 drops liquid stevia

PER SERVING
Calories: 306;
Fat: 26g;
Saturated Fat: 4g;
Sodium: 126mg;
Total Carbohydrates: 17g;
Net Carbohydrates: 9g;
Fiber: 8g;
Sugar: 5g;
Protein: 9g

TO MAKE THE TAHINI SAUCE

1. Put the water, cilantro, tahini, lemon juice, vinegar, garlic powder, salt, and liquid stevia in a blender, and purée until smooth, scraping down the sides as needed.

2. To serve, divide the vegetables among 4 serving bowls, and drizzle with the tahini sauce.

INGREDIENT TIP: Tahini (ground sesame seeds) is what gives hummus its rich, savory flavor. I recommend choosing an organic tahini for the best flavor. It really does make a difference. Once you have a jar of it in your refrigerator, you'll find all kinds of uses for it. I even prefer it to almond butter in my morning smoothies.

Coconut Curry Vegetables and Tofu

DAIRY-FREE, GLUTEN-FREE, NUT-FREE, VEGAN

Serves 4 | **PREP TIME:** 10 minutes | **COOK TIME:** 20 minutes

Coconut curry is an easy and tasty way to clean out your refrigerator. This version is similar to the Green Curry Shrimp and Vegetables (page 86) but opts for a different variety of vegetables and tofu. As in many recipes that use tofu, it's pressed first to remove some of the water. This way, it will hold its shape when cooked.

1 (14-ounce) block firm or extra-firm tofu, cut in half and pressed (see tip)

2 tablespoons canola oil, divided

1 onion, halved and sliced

1 tablespoon minced garlic

1 tablespoon minced fresh ginger

4 tablespoons red curry paste

4 cups vegetable broth

1 (14-ounce) can coconut milk

1 red bell pepper, cut into 2-inch strips

1 green bell pepper, cut into 2-inch strips

1 small head broccoli, cut into florets

1 large carrot, cut into rounds

PER SERVING
Calories: 526;
Fat: 41g;
Saturated Fat: 24g;
Sodium: 1608mg;
Total Carbohydrates: 25g;
Net Carbohydrates: 17g;
Fiber: 8g;
Sugar: 11g;
Protein: 19g

1. Preheat the oven to 425°F. Line a rimmed baking sheet with parchment paper.
2. Cut the pressed tofu into 1-inch cubes. In a large bowl, gently toss the cubes with 1 tablespoon of oil, being careful not to break them. Spread onto the baking sheet. Season with salt.
3. Transfer the baking sheet to the oven, and bake for 13 minutes, or until gently browned.
4. Flip, then bake for 4 minutes to brown the other side.
5. Meanwhile, heat a large pot over medium heat, then pour in the remaining 1 tablespoon of oil, and tilt to coat. Add the onion, and cook for 2 to 3 minutes, or until beginning to soften. Add the garlic, ginger, and curry paste and cook for 1 minute, or until fragrant.
6. Add the vegetable broth and coconut milk, and bring to a simmer; cook for 2 minutes. Add the bell peppers, broccoli, and carrot, and simmer for 5 minutes, or until the broccoli is just tender.
7. Stir in the tofu, and serve.

INGREDIENT TIP: To press the tofu, place the tofu halves on a cutting board set atop a kitchen towel. Top with a second cutting board, then top that with several books or another heavy object, such as a cast-iron pan. Let sit for at least 10 minutes, or longer if you have the time. The liquid from the tofu will seep out the sides and soak into the towel.

Vegetarian **103**

Spicy Tofu and Swiss Chard Stir-Fry

DAIRY-FREE, NUT-FREE, VEGAN

Serves 4 | **PREP TIME:** 10 minutes | **COOK TIME:** 20 minutes

Toasted sesame oil, dry sherry, and loads of fresh garlic and ginger add depth and complexity to this stir-fry. Sugar, honey, or orange juice are typical sweeteners in stir-fry sauces, but I opt for liquid stevia. Feel free to use whatever non-nutritive sweetener you like. I suggest Swiss chard here, but another sturdy leafy green vegetable will also work, such as collard greens or bok choy.

1 (14-ounce) block firm or extra-firm tofu, cut in half and pressed (see page 103)

2 tablespoons canola oil, divided

Sea salt

1 tablespoon toasted sesame oil

1 small red onion, halved and thinly sliced

1 bunch Swiss chard, stems thinly sliced, leaves chopped

1 tablespoon minced garlic

1 teaspoon minced fresh ginger

¼ teaspoon red pepper flakes

¼ cup low-sodium soy sauce

2 tablespoons dry sherry or dry white wine

2 or 3 drops liquid stevia

2 scallions, green and white parts thinly sliced on a bias

2 tablespoons toasted sesame seeds

1. Preheat the oven to 425°F. Line a rimmed baking sheet with parchment paper.

2. Cut the pressed tofu into 1-inch cubes. In a large bowl, gently toss the cubes with 1 tablespoon of canola oil, being careful not to break them. Spread onto the baking sheet. Season with salt.

3. Transfer the baking sheet to the oven, and bake for 13 minutes, or until gently browned.

4. Flip, then bake for 4 minutes to brown the other side.

5. Meanwhile, heat a large skillet over high heat until hot, then pour in the remaining 1 tablespoon of canola oil and the toasted sesame oil, and tilt to coat the bottom.

6. Add the onion, and sauté for 4 minutes, or until beginning to brown.

7. Reduce the heat to medium. Add the Swiss chard stems, and cook for 2 to 3 minutes, or until just beginning to soften.

8. Add the garlic, ginger, and red pepper flakes, and cook for 1 minute.

9. In a small bowl, whisk the soy sauce, sherry, and liquid stevia.

PER SERVING
Calories: 244;
Fat: 17g;
Saturated Fat: 2g;
Sodium: 971mg;
Total Carbohydrates: 9g;
Net Carbohydrates: 6g;
Fiber: 3g;
Sugar: 2g;
Protein: 11g

10. Add the Swiss chard leaves, scallions, and soy sauce mixture to the skillet. Simmer, stirring frequently, about 5 minutes, or until the Swiss chard is wilted.

11. Carefully fold the tofu into the vegetables, and stir to mix. Sprinkle with the sesame seeds.

COOKING TIP: When you're cooking with fresh garlic, it helps to have a silicone garlic peeler. Simply place each clove inside, and roll it with the palm of your hand. If you don't have one, place the whole clove on a cutting board, and gently press it with the flat side of a chef's knife. This will loosen the peel enough to remove it.

Tofu Tikka Masala

DAIRY-FREE, GLUTEN-FREE, NUT-FREE, VEGAN

Serves 4 | **PREP TIME:** 10 minutes | **COOK TIME:** 20 minutes

The origins of tikka masala, a spicy curry featuring tomatoes, turmeric, and cream, are unclear—maybe India, maybe Great Britain, maybe immigrant chefs from Bangladesh who created "Indian" food in their new home. Whatever its origins, it was one of my favorite dishes while living in England. On foggy days the bright, tangy sauce was just what I needed. This version takes the familiar flavors in a plant-based direction with tofu and coconut cream. In this recipe you pop the cubed tofu straight into the curry, but you can also roast it first—just follow steps 1 through 4 of Spicy Tofu and Swiss Chard Stir-Fry (page 104).

1 (14-ounce) block firm or
    extra-firm tofu, cut in half
    and pressed (see page 103)
2 tablespoons canola oil
1 small onion, diced
2 large garlic cloves, minced
1 (1-inch) piece fresh
    ginger, minced
2 teaspoons garam masala
2 teaspoons ground turmeric
1 teaspoon ground coriander
¼ teaspoon red pepper flakes
1 (15-ounce) can tomato sauce
1 cup vegetable broth
1 cup coconut cream
¼ cup tomato paste
Sea salt
Freshly ground black pepper
Small handful fresh cilantro,
    coarsely chopped

1. Cut the pressed tofu into 1-inch cubes.
2. Heat a large pot over medium heat until hot, then pour in the oil, and tilt to coat the bottom.
3. Add the onion, garlic, and ginger, and cook for 5 minutes, or until somewhat softened.
4. Add the garam masala, turmeric, coriander, and red pepper flakes, and cook for 30 seconds to 1 minute, or just until fragrant.
5. Add the tomato sauce, vegetable broth, coconut cream, and tomato paste, and bring to a simmer. Season with salt and pepper.

PER SERVING
Calories: 378;
Fat: 30g;
Saturated Fat: 19g;
Sodium: 312mg;
Total Carbohydrates: 20g;
Net Carbohydrates: 16g;
Fiber: 4g;
Sugar: 9g;
Protein: 12g

6. Add the tofu, and cook for 10 minutes, to allow the tofu to soak up all the awesome flavors in the sauce.

7. To serve, divide among 4 serving bowls, and top with the cilantro.

Energizing Tofu and Veggie Noodle Bowl

DAIRY-FREE, VEGAN

Serves 4 | **PREP TIME:** 10 minutes | **COOK TIME:** 15 minutes

Vibrant purple cabbage, fragrant fresh herbs, and spiralized carrot and cucumber noodles make this healthy bowl a rainbow of colors and flavors. It's served with a fresh soy-ginger dressing that has become a staple in my kitchen. Whenever I'm looking for bold Asian flavors, this dressing is my go-to. Toasted cashews are slightly higher in carbohydrates than other nuts, but they're still decidedly in the low-carb territory. If you prefer, you can swap in toasted slivered almonds or even a couple of tablespoons of toasted sesame seeds.

1 (14-ounce) block firm or extra-firm tofu, cut in half and pressed (see page 103)

2 tablespoons toasted sesame oil, divided

Sea salt

¼ cup low-sodium soy sauce

2 tablespoons freshly squeezed lime juice

1 teaspoon sambal oelek or another chili paste

1 teaspoon minced fresh ginger

1 or 2 drops liquid stevia

½ head purple cabbage, cored and thinly sliced

2 carrots, spiralized or cut into ribbons

1. Preheat the oven to 425°F. Line a rimmed baking sheet with parchment paper.
2. Cut the pressed tofu into 1-inch cubes. In a large bowl, gently toss the cubes with 1 tablespoon of sesame oil, being careful not to break them. Spread onto the baking sheet. Season with salt.
3. Transfer the baking sheet to the oven, and bake for 13 minutes, or until gently browned.
4. Flip, then bake for 4 minutes to brown the other side.
5. Meanwhile, to make the dressing, in a small bowl, whisk the remaining 1 tablespoon of sesame oil, soy sauce, lime juice, sambal oelek, ginger, and liquid stevia.

2 cucumbers, peeled and
   spiralized or cut into ribbons
½ cup chopped fresh basil
½ cup chopped fresh cilantro
¼ cup chopped fresh mint
¼ cup chopped
   toasted cashews

PER SERVING
Calories: 221;
Fat: 13g;
Saturated Fat: 2g;
Sodium: 997mg;
Total Carbohydrates: 20g;
Net Carbohydrates: 14g;
Fiber: 6g;
Sugar: 8g;
Protein: 13g

6. Put the cabbage, carrots, cucumbers, basil, cilantro, and mint in a large mixing bowl. Drizzle with the dressing, and toss gently to mix.

7. Divide the salad among 4 serving plates. Top with the roasted tofu, and sprinkle with toasted cashews.

INGREDIENT TIP: If you have organic cucumbers, there's no need to peel them. The peel is a good source of fiber and vitamin K.

Blackened Tofu with Cheesy "Grits"

GLUTEN-FREE, VEGETARIAN

Serves 4 | **PREP TIME:** 10 minutes | **COOK TIME:** 20 minutes

Did you know you can still enjoy "grits" on a low-carb diet? This version makes use of the usual low-carb standby, cauliflower, but adds an extra layer of texture from almond flour. Without the starch in corn grits, this version gets its creaminess from a splash of heavy cream and a generous handful of Cheddar cheese. This Southern comfort food is delicious with blackened tofu and Oven-Roasted Brussels Sprouts (page 30), which you can make at the same time you roast the tofu.

1 (14-ounce) block firm or extra-firm tofu, cut in half and pressed (see page 103)

2 tablespoons blackening spice blend (see tip)

2 tablespoons extra-virgin olive oil, divided

1 small head cauliflower, cored and cut into florets

½ cup almond flour

1 tablespoon butter

Sea salt

2 tablespoons heavy cream

1 cup Cheddar cheese

1. Preheat the oven to 425°F. Line a rimmed baking sheet with parchment paper.
2. Cut the pressed tofu into 1-inch cubes.
3. In a large bowl, gently toss the tofu with the blackening spice mix until well coated, then toss with 1 tablespoon of the oil being careful not to break the cubes. Spread onto the baking sheet.
4. Transfer the baking sheet to the oven, and bake for 13 minutes, or until gently browned.
5. Flip, then bake for 4 minutes to brown the other side.
6. Meanwhile, put the cauliflower in a food processor fitted with the standard blade, and pulse until finely chopped.
7. Add the almond flour, and pulse once or twice, until just combined.
8. Heat a large deep skillet over medium-high heat until hot, then pour in the remaining 1 tablespoon of oil, and melt the butter. (A cast-iron skillet works well here.) Tilt to coat the bottom.
9. Add the cauliflower mixture, season with salt, and cook for 5 minutes, or until soft.

PER SERVING
Calories: 353;
Fat: 29g;
Saturated Fat: 12g;
Sodium: 292mg;
Total Carbohydrates: 7g;
Net Carbohydrates: 4g;
Fiber: 3g;
Sugar: 2g;
Protein: 18g

10. Stir in the heavy cream, and cook for 1 minute.

11. Remove the skillet from the heat, and stir in the cheese.

12. Divide the "grits" among 4 serving bowls. Top with the blackened tofu.

INGREDIENT TIP: To make your own blackening spice mix, combine 1 tablespoon smoked paprika, 1 teaspoon garlic powder, ½ teaspoon onion powder, ½ teaspoon dried thyme, ½ teaspoon dried oregano, ½ teaspoon sea salt, ¼ teaspoon cayenne pepper, and ¼ teaspoon black pepper. This makes just enough of the spice blend for this recipe. Or upsize it and make a batch that you can use in other dishes.

Blueberry, Almond, and Cream Cheese
Coffee Cake, page 127

7

desserts

Bulletproof Hot Chocolate

GLUTEN-FREE, NUT-FREE, SOY-FREE, VEGETARIAN

Serves 1 | **PREP TIME:** 2 minutes

Taking a cue from bulletproof coffee—a favorite among low-carb and keto dieters—this tasty hot chocolate is made with butter and boiling water. Use an immersion blender to whip it up into frothy hot chocolate perfection. You could also use coconut oil if you prefer a dairy-free version. Make an adult hot chocolate by adding a shot of dark rum or whiskey or another liquor that doesn't contain added sugar.

2 tablespoons butter

1 tablespoon unsweetened cocoa powder

2 teaspoons Swerve or another granulated non-nutritive sweetener

¼ teaspoon pure vanilla extract

1 cup boiling water

In a 2-cup glass measuring cup, mix the butter, cocoa powder, Swerve, vanilla, and water. Use an immersion blender to blend until frothy. Enjoy immediately.

> **INGREDIENT TIP:** Use salted butter or add a tiny pinch sea salt to bring out the flavors in the chocolate.

PER SERVING
Calories: 219;
Fat: 24g;
Saturated Fat: 15g;
Sodium: 165mg;
Total Carbohydrates: 3g;
Net Carbohydrates: 1g;
Fiber: 2g;
Sugar: 0g;
Protein: 1g

Deconstructed Cannoli Cups

GLUTEN-FREE, NUT-FREE, SOY-FREE, VEGETARIAN

Serves 4 | **PREP TIME:** 5 minutes

Forgo the fried pastry shell, and enjoy traditional cannoli filling on its own in these sweet dessert cups. Cacao nibs are simply roasted cocoa beans without any added sugar. They're crunchy and slightly bitter, but in a good way. I love the texture they bring to this dish and often add them to my morning smoothies or stir them into brownie batter. To make a vegan version of this dessert, use a plant-based ricotta, such as Kite Hill.

1 pound whole-milk
   ricotta cheese

¼ cup cacao nibs

2 tablespoons Swerve or
   another granulated
   non-nutritive sweetener

1 teaspoon orange zest

¼ teaspoon ground cinnamon

PER SERVING
Calories: 247;
Fat: 17g;
Saturated Fat: 9g;
Sodium: 214mg;
Total Carbohydrates: 11g;
Net Carbohydrates: 7g;
Fiber: 4g;
Sugar: 6g;
Protein: 14g

1. In a medium mixing bowl, gently mix the ricotta cheese, cocoa nibs, Swerve, orange zest, and cinnamon together. Divide among 4 serving cups.

2. Chill for at least 10 minutes before serving.

INGREDIENT TIP: Look for a good-quality ricotta cheese or even consider making your own. It's not as difficult as it sounds, and there are numerous tutorials online. The flavor is far superior to store-bought ricotta.

Cherry Cheesecake Smoothie Bowl

GLUTEN-FREE, SOY-FREE, VEGETARIAN

Serves 4 | **PREP TIME:** 5 minutes

Here's another deconstructed dessert. It takes all the flavors of baked cherry cheesecake and delivers them in a low-carb smoothie bowl—no baking required. As strange as it sounds, consider topping this smoothie bowl with a pinch of flaky sea salt, such as fleur de sel. It adds a nice textural contrast, and the salt amplifies the other flavors. You'll find plenty of uses for flaky sea salt in your kitchen.

1 cup frozen tart cherries

8 ounces cream cheese, softened

½ to 1 cup milk

¼ cup Swerve or another granulated non-nutritive sweetener

1 teaspoon pure vanilla extract

2 tablespoons cacao nibs

2 tablespoons slivered toasted almonds

Pinch flaky sea salt

1. Put the cherries, cream cheese, ½ cup of milk, Swerve, and vanilla in a blender, and purée until smooth, scraping down the sides and adding more milk as needed to get your blender going.

2. Divide the mixture among 4 serving cups, and top with the cacao nibs, almonds, and salt.

PER SERVING
Calories: 287;
Fat: 23g;
Saturated Fat: 14g;
Sodium: 256mg;
Total Carbohydrates: 13g;
Net Carbohydrates: 9g;
Fiber: 4g;
Sugar: 7g;
Protein: 8g

Key Lime Pie Truffles

GLUTEN-FREE, SOY-FREE, VEGETARIAN

Makes 16 truffles | **PREP TIME:** 25 minutes

These zesty little truffles are a perfect portion-controlled solution to Key lime pie cravings. They're creamy, tangy, and lightly sweetened with stevia on the inside, with a sea salt and toasted coconut crust on the outside. Make sure you have some friends around to share them with so you don't "accidentally" eat them all in one sitting. If you can't find Key limes, use a combination of fresh lime juice and fresh Meyer lemon juice, which has a similar floral quality to Key limes.

8 ounces cream cheese, softened

2 tablespoons freshly squeezed lime juice, ideally from Key limes

1 teaspoon lime zest

6 or 7 drops liquid stevia

¼ cup shredded toasted coconut

¼ cup macadamia nuts

¼ teaspoon coarse sea salt

**PER SERVING
(2 TRUFFLES)**
Calories: 139;
Fat: 14g;
Saturated Fat: 8g;
Sodium: 145mg;
Total Carbohydrates: 2g;
Net Carbohydrates: 1g;
Fiber: 1g;
Sugar: 1g;
Protein: 3g

1. In a medium mixing bowl, mix the cream cheese, lime juice and zest, and liquid stevia until well combined. Put in the freezer to chill for 10 minutes.

2. Meanwhile, put the coconut, macadamia nuts, and sea salt in a food processor, and pulse until finely ground. Transfer to a shallow dish.

3. Scoop the cream cheese mixture out of the bowl with a 1-tablespoon measuring spoon, and roll in the coconut mixture. Set in a storage container. Repeat to make 16 truffles. Refrigerate for 15 minutes before serving. Store in the refrigerator.

Coconut Lime Paletas

DAIRY-FREE, GLUTEN-FREE, NUT-FREE, SOY-FREE, VEGAN

Serves 6 | **PREP TIME:** 5 minutes

I live in a neighborhood with a thriving Latino community, and we're lucky enough to have a specialty grocery store with all kinds of spices, herbs, and vegetables you just don't find in most mainstream ones. Whenever I go shopping, my kids always beg for the paletas (Mexican ice pops) sold near the cash register. Many are fruit-based, but they still have a lot of added sugar that I would prefer not to serve to the kids. This version is tart, creamy, and sweet and satisfies their cravings—and mine, too!

1 (14-ounce) can full-fat coconut milk

¼ cup Swerve or another granulated non-nutritive sweetener

¼ cup freshly squeezed lime juice

1 teaspoon lime zest

PER SERVING
Calories: 156;
Fat: 16g;
Saturated Fat: 14g;
Sodium: 10mg;
Total Carbohydrates: 5g;
Net Carbohydrates: 3g;
Fiber: 2g;
Sugar: 3g;
Protein: 2g

1. Put the coconut milk, Swerve, and lime juice and zest in a blender, and purée until smooth, scraping down the sides as needed.
2. Pour into 5 or 6 ice pop molds (the number will depend on how large each is). Freeze until solid.

VARIATION TIP: To make a chocolate paleta, substitute half-and-half for the coconut milk and 3 ounces 80-percent cacao chocolate for the lime juice and zest. Heat this in a small saucepan over low heat, stirring until the chocolate is completely melted. Stir in the Swerve. Cool before pouring into the ice pop molds.

Coconut Peppermint Patties

DAIRY-FREE, GLUTEN-FREE, NUT-FREE, SOY-FREE, VEGAN

Serves 24 | **PREP TIME:** 25 minutes

These refreshing sweets are a cross between Mounds bars and York Peppermint Patties. The filling is made with shredded coconut, sugar-free maple syrup, and peppermint extract, and it's coated in a thick layer of dark chocolate. The trick to making these treats hold together is thoroughly processing the coconut in a food processor. It should stay clumped when you press it with your hands. If not, pulse it a bit more.

3 cups shredded unsweetened coconut flakes

½ cup sugar-free maple syrup, sweetened with monk fruit

¼ cup coconut oil, melted

½ teaspoon peppermint extract

6 ounces 80-percent cacao chocolate

1 tablespoon nonhydrogenated shortening

**PER SERVING
(1 PEPPERMINT PATTY)**
Calories: 147;
Fat: 14g;
Saturated Fat: 11g;
Sodium: 5mg;
Total Carbohydrates: 6g;
Net Carbohydrates: 3g;
Fiber: 3g;
Sugar: 3g;
Protein: 1g

1. Put the coconut flakes in a food processor, and process until finely ground and nearly holding together.

2. Add the maple syrup, coconut oil, and peppermint extract, and process until the mixture easily clumps together.

3. Form the mixture into small cookies, and place on a rimmed baking sheet lined with parchment paper. Put in the freezer, and chill for about 15 minutes, or until firm.

4. Meanwhile, in a heavy-bottomed skillet, heat the chocolate and shortening over very low heat until nearly melted, stirring occasionally.

5. Remove the pan from the heat. Carefully dip each of the chilled coconut cookies into the dark chocolate mixture, turning to coat both sides.

6. Put the cookies back on the baking sheet, and chill for 5 minutes in the freezer. Store in the refrigerator.

COOKING TIP: Another option for melting the chocolate is to do it in a double boiler, which is one pan or heat-proof bowl set over a pot of barely simmering water. This is a gentler method of heat than cooking directly on the stovetop. But it's a hassle, so if you have a heavy-bottomed skillet, it's easier. Just keep an eye on the chocolate, and remove it from the heat before it's fully melted.

Chocolate Peanut Butter Cups

DAIRY-FREE, GLUTEN-FREE, SOY-FREE, VEGAN

Makes 12 (1-cup) servings | **PREP TIME:** 5 minutes

These little sweets are just like the chocolaty, peanut buttery treats of your childhood, with one important distinction: They don't have any added sugar, so they won't send your blood sugar skyrocketing. Because they don't contain all the additives of packaged chocolates, these are best kept in the refrigerator. I actually have come to prefer them that way, because the cold brings out different flavors in the chocolate.

¾ cup creamy salted natural peanut butter

½ cup coconut oil, melted

½ cup unsweetened cocoa powder

5 to 7 drops liquid stevia

PER SERVING
Calories: 181;
Fat: 18g;
Saturated Fat: 10g;
Sodium: 75mg;
Total Carbohydrates: 5g;
Net Carbohydrates: 3g;
Fiber: 2g;
Sugar: 2g;
Protein: 5g

1. In a small bowl, combine the peanut butter, coconut oil, cocoa powder, and liquid stevia, and whisk until thoroughly integrated. If you have an immersion blender, that makes the process even easier.
2. Add more liquid stevia as needed until it reaches your desired level of sweetness.
3. Pour the mixture into a muffin tin lined with circles cut from parchment paper.
4. Refrigerate until set, about 30 minutes. Serve chilled. Store in the refrigerator.

COOKING TIP: If the peanut butter is too stiff to integrate with the other ingredients, warm it in the microwave briefly, just until softened.

Peanut Butter Cookie Dough

GLUTEN-FREE, SOY-FREE, VEGETARIAN

Makes 1 cup cookie dough or 16 dough balls | **PREP TIME:** 15 minutes

As a child, my favorite indulgence was sneaking out to the large freezer in my parents' garage, where they kept "the good stuff." For me, that was frozen cookie dough, which they bought in bulk from a restaurant supplier. (I have no idea why, since the rest of our diet was pretty healthy—but I loved it.) It had the perfect balance of salty and sweet that I craved. I ignored the risk of salmonella, of course. But looking back, that may not have been so wise. Not only did it feed my sugar addiction, but it also put me at risk for a no-nonsense foodborne illness. Now I go for a much safer and healthier option—and it still has that salty-sweet decadence.

¼ cup coconut oil, melted

¼ cup butter, softened

½ cup creamy salted natural peanut butter

6 or 7 drops liquid stevia

2 tablespoons Swerve or another granulated non-nutritive sweetener

PER SERVING
Calories: 150;
Fat: 15g;
Saturated Fat: 6g;
Sodium: 75mg;
Total Carbohydrates: 4g;
Net Carbohydrates: 2g;
Fiber: 2g;
Sugar: 1g;
Protein: 4g

1. In a small mixing bowl, combine the coconut oil, butter, peanut butter, and liquid stevia, and whisk until thoroughly integrated.
2. Put the bowl in the refrigerator to firm up.
3. Use a 1-tablespoon measuring spoon to scoop the dough out of the bowl. Roll it in the Swerve, and set in a storage container. Return to the refrigerator for 10 minutes to firm up. You can even put these in the freezer for a firmer texture—all of the fat will keep them from turning rock hard.

Chocolate Mousse

GLUTEN-FREE, NUT-FREE, SOY-FREE, VEGETARIAN

Serves 8 | **PREP TIME:** 15 minutes | **COOK TIME:** 5 minutes, plus chilling time

Don't let the short ingredient list fool you; this sweet dessert is so delicious and intensely chocolaty. Top it with crème fraîche and a handful of raspberries, or freeze it in a small baking dish lined with parchment paper, and cut into squares. I should mention that this dish uses raw eggs, as most mousses do. Consuming raw or undercooked eggs does increase your risk of foodborne illness. If raw eggs make you a little squeamish, I get it. Just triple the amount of whipping cream, and skip the eggs.

4 ounces good-quality dark
   chocolate, at least
   80-percent cacao
2 tablespoons butter
3 large eggs, separated
1 or 2 drops freshly squeezed
   lemon juice
½ cup heavy cream
2 tablespoons Swerve or
   another granulated
   non-nutritive sweetener
¼ teaspoon sea salt
1 teaspoon pure vanilla extract

PER SERVING
Calories: 183;
Fat: 15g;
Saturated Fat: 9g;
Sodium: 108mg;
Total Carbohydrates: 8g;
Net Carbohydrates: 6g;
Fiber: 2g;
Sugar: 4g;
Protein: 3g

1. In a heavy-bottomed skillet or a double boiler, heat the dark chocolate and butter over low heat for about 3 minutes, or until just melted. Set aside to cool.

2. In a large mixing bowl, using a whisk or electric mixer, beat the egg whites and lemon juice until stiff peaks form.

3. In another large mixing bowl, using clean beaters, beat the heavy cream and Swerve until soft peaks form.

4. Stir the egg yolks, salt, and vanilla into the cooled chocolate mixture, then fold in half of the whipped cream.

5. Pour the chocolate mixture into the whipped egg whites along with the remaining whipped cream, and fold in until just mixed. Try not to overmix, or you will lose some of the volume.

6. Divide the mousse among 8 serving cups, and put in the refrigerator until chilled. To speed this up, put in the freezer, and serve in about 10 minutes.

COOKING TIP: You can use ⅛ teaspoon cream of tartar instead of the lemon juice if you wish. I find that I rarely have it in my pantry, so I just use lemon juice. The acid helps to beat more volume into the egg whites.

Low-Carb Lemon Bars

GLUTEN-FREE, SOY-FREE, VEGETARIAN

Serves 12 | **PREP TIME:** 10 minutes | **COOK TIME:** 7 minutes, plus 23 minutes to chill

Growing up, my best friend, Marcella, and I would bake pans of lemon bars or Rice Krispies treats and eat until our tummies hurt or until half of the pan was gone—whichever came second. I marvel at how we didn't both end up in the dentist's chair more often. These days, since I don't really indulge in sugar anymore—and frankly, have much lower expectations of how sweet something should taste—lemon bars have become a distant memory. Thankfully, with their savory, barely sweet crust and tart lemony filling, these low-carb bars bring back all of those delicious memories.

¾ cup butter, divided

2 cups almond flour

⅓ cup plus 2 tablespoons Swerve or another granulated non-nutritive sweetener

½ teaspoon sea salt

5 large egg yolks

½ cup freshly squeezed lemon juice

2 teaspoons lemon zest

2 tablespoons unflavored gelatin

1. Preheat the oven to 350°F.

2. In a small saucepan, melt all the butter. Remove from the heat. Remove ¼ cup of it with a measuring cup.

3. Put the almond flour, 2 tablespoons of Swerve, salt, and the ¼ cup of melted butter in a food processor, and pulse a couple of times, just until integrated and the mixture starts to come together.

4. Transfer the mixture to an 8-by-8-inch baking dish, and use your palms to flatten it, pressing all the way to the edges.

5. Transfer the baking dish to the oven, and bake for 8 minutes, or until beginning to brown.

6. Meanwhile, add the remaining ⅓ cup of Swerve, egg yolks, and lemon juice and zest to the saucepan with the remaining ½ cup of butter, which should have cooled slightly.

7. Return the saucepan to low heat, and cook until the curd thickens, whisking constantly. This should take about 8 minutes, depending on the heat. Don't rush it, but if the curd isn't thickening, increase the heat slightly.

continued on next page...

PER SERVING
Calories: 187;
Fat: 18g;
Saturated Fat: 8g;
Sodium: 171mg;
Total Carbohydrates: 3g;
Net Carbohydrates: 2g;
Fiber: 1g;
Sugar: 0g;
Protein: 4g

8. Whisk the gelatin into 2 tablespoons of water, then pour it into the curd, and whisk until thoroughly mixed.

9. Pour the curd over the baked crust, spreading it out with a spatula, and return the baking dish to the oven. Bake for 12 to 15 minutes, or until set. The center will still jiggle slightly.

INGREDIENT TIP: If you can find Meyer lemons, use them in this recipe. They yield more juice than regular lemons, and have a slight floral aroma.

Almond Flour Brownies

GLUTEN-FREE, SOY-FREE, VEGETARIAN

Serves 9 | **PREP TIME:** 10 minutes | **COOK TIME:** 20 minutes

I use a combination of bittersweet chocolate and cocoa powder because the chocolate bar contains chocolate and fat, which keeps the brownies moist and gives them a deep chocolate flavor. The cocoa powder helps absorb some of the moisture in the recipe and, along with the almond flour, works as a substitute for traditional wheat flour.

½ cup butter

6 ounces bittersweet chocolate

1 cup almond flour

1 cup Swerve or another
   granulated non-nutritive
   sweetener

¼ cup unsweetened
   cocoa powder

1 teaspoon sea salt

½ teaspoon baking powder

3 large eggs, whisked

1 tablespoon pure
   vanilla extract

PER SERVING
Calories: 273;
Fat: 23g;
Saturated Fat: 12g;
Sodium: 303mg;
Total Carbohydrates: 11g;
Net Carbohydrates: 8g;
Fiber: 3g;
Sugar: 5g;
Protein: 6g

1. Preheat the oven to 350°F. Line an 8-by-8-inch baking dish with parchment paper.

2. Put the butter and bittersweet chocolate in a small saucepan over low heat, and stir until melted. Remove from the heat, and let cool somewhat.

3. In a bowl, combine the almond flour, Swerve, cocoa powder, salt, and baking powder.

4. Pour the melted chocolate and butter, eggs, and vanilla into the bowl, and stir until completely mixed.

5. Press the mixture into the baking dish, transfer to the oven, and bake for 18 to 20 minutes, or until just set. I like to keep them on the slightly squidgy side.

COOKING TIP: Make sure to let the melted chocolate and butter mixture cool so you don't cook the eggs when you mix them together.

Everyday Vanilla Cheesecake

GLUTEN-FREE, SOY-FREE, VEGETARIAN

Serves 8 | **PREP TIME:** 5 minutes | **COOK TIME:** 7 minutes, plus 23 minutes to chill

This dessert bridges the gap between a no-bake cheesecake made with graham crackers and a traditional cheesecake. Here, the almond flour crust gets quick-baked, then it's topped with a creamy filling. This means you can satisfy your cravings for cheesecake in a fraction of the time it usually takes to bake a one.

2 cups almond flour

¼ cup butter, melted

⅓ cup plus 2 tablespoons Swerve or another granulated non-nutritive sweetener

½ teaspoon sea salt

2 (8-ounce) packages cream cheese, softened

½ cup heavy cream

2 tablespoons freshly squeezed lemon juice

1 teaspoon pure vanilla extract

PER SERVING
Calories: 344;
Fat: 34g;
Saturated Fat: 18g;
Sodium: 301mg;
Total Carbohydrates: 5g;
Net Carbohydrates: 4g;
Fiber: 1g;
Sugar: 0g;
Protein: 7g

1. Preheat the oven to 350°F.

2. Put the almond flour, butter, 2 tablespoons of Swerve, and the salt in a food processor, and pulse a couple of times, just until integrated and the mixture starts to come together.

3. Transfer the mixture to an 8- or 9-inch springform pan, and use your palms to flatten it, pressing all the way to the edges.

4. Transfer the pan to the oven, and bake for 7 minutes, then put in the refrigerator to cool for 8 minutes.

5. While the crust bakes and cools, in a large mixing bowl, combine the remaining ⅓ cup of Swerve, the cream cheese, heavy cream, lemon juice, and vanilla. Beat with an electric mixer or a wooden spoon until smooth.

6. Spread the filling onto the cooled almond flour crust, and put the pan in the freezer for at least 15 minutes to firm up. Alternately, chill in the refrigerator for 1 hour before serving.

Blueberry, Almond, and Cream Cheese Coffee Cake

GLUTEN-FREE, SOY-FREE, VEGETARIAN

Serves 8 | **PREP TIME:** 10 minutes | **COOK TIME:** 20 minutes

Decadent doesn't even begin to describe this coffee cake. That's why it's here, in the dessert section, instead of at the front of the book with the breakfast recipes. But I won't tell anyone if you want to serve it for breakfast. It's especially yummy with afternoon tea or coffee.

2 cups almond flour

½ cup Swerve or another granulated non-nutritive sweetener

3 tablespoons coconut flour

1½ teaspoons baking powder

¼ teaspoon baking soda

2 large eggs

⅓ cup butter, softened

⅓ cup milk

1 tablespoon pure vanilla extract

1 cup blueberries

1 (8-ounce) package cream cheese, cut into 1-inch pieces

¼ cup slivered toasted almonds

1. Preheat the oven to 375°F. Line an 8-by-8-inch baking dish with parchment paper.
2. In a large mixing bowl, combine the almond flour, Swerve, coconut flour, baking powder, and baking soda.
3. Add the eggs, butter, milk, and vanilla, and stir just until mixed.
4. Fold in the blueberries and cream cheese. Spread this mixture into the baking dish, and top with the almonds.
5. Bake for 20 minutes, or until completely set and beginning to brown around the edges.

PER SERVING
Calories: 315;
Fat: 27g;
Saturated Fat: 13g;
Sodium: 203mg;
Total Carbohydrates: 12g;
Net Carbohydrates: 8g;
Fiber: 4g;
Sugar: 3g;
Protein: 8g

Coconut Peppermint Patties, page 119

THE DIRTY DOZEN AND
THE CLEAN FIFTEEN™

A nonprofit environmental watchdog organization called Environmental Working Group (EWG) looks at data supplied by the US Department of Agriculture (USDA) and the Food and Drug Administration (FDA) about pesticide residues. Each year it compiles a list of the best and worst pesticide loads found in commercial crops. You can use these lists to decide which fruits and vegetables to buy organic to minimize your exposure to pesticides and which produce is considered safe enough to buy conventionally. This does not mean they are pesticide-free, though, so wash these fruits and vegetables thoroughly. You can find the list online at EWG.org/FoodNews.

Dirty Dozen™

1. strawberries
2. spinach
3. kale
4. nectarines
5. apples
6. grapes
7. peaches
8. cherries
9. pears
10. tomatoes
11. celery
12. potatoes
→ Additionally, nearly ¾ of hot pepper samples contained pesticide residues.

Clean Fifteen™

1. avocados
2. sweet corn
3. pineapples
4. sweet peas (frozen)
5. onions
6. papayas
7. eggplants
8. asparagus
9. kiwis
10. cabbages
11. cauliflower
12. cantaloupes
13. broccoli
14. mushrooms
15. honeydew melons

MEASUREMENTS AND CONVERSIONS

VOLUME EQUIVALENTS (LIQUID)

US STANDARD	US STANDARD (OUNCES)	METRIC (APPROXIMATE)
2 tablespoons	1 fl. oz.	30 mL
¼ cup	2 fl. oz.	60 mL
½ cup	4 fl. oz.	120 mL
1 cup	8 fl. oz.	240 mL
1½ cups	12 fl. oz.	355 mL
2 cups or 1 pint	16 fl. oz.	475 mL
4 cups or 1 quart	32 fl. oz.	1 L
1 gallon	128 fl. oz.	4 L

VOLUME EQUIVALENTS (DRY)

US STANDARD	METRIC (APPROXIMATE)
⅛ teaspoon	0.5 mL
¼ teaspoon	1 mL
½ teaspoon	2 mL
¾ teaspoon	4 mL
1 teaspoon	5 mL
1 tablespoon	15 mL
¼ cup	59 mL
⅓ cup	79 mL
½ cup	118 mL
⅔ cup	156 mL
¾ cup	177 mL
1 cup	235 mL
2 cups or 1 pint	475 mL
3 cups	700 mL
4 cups or 1 quart	1 L

OVEN TEMPERATURES

FAHRENHEIT	CELSIUS (APPROXIMATE)
250°F	120°C
300°F	150°C
325°F	165°C
350°F	180°C
375°F	190°C
400°F	200°C
425°F	220°C
450°F	230°C

WEIGHT EQUIVALENTS

US STANDARD	METRIC (APPROXIMATE)
½ ounce	15 g
1 ounce	30 g
2 ounces	60 g
4 ounces	115 g
8 ounces	225 g
12 ounces	340 g
16 ounces or 1 pound	455 g

References

Atkins. "Atkins 20®: An Effective Diet for Weight Loss." Accessed March 20, 2019.
https://www.atkins.com/how-it-works/atkins-20.

Cefalu, William T., et al. "Effect of Chromium Picolinate on Insulin Sensitivity in Vivo."
The Journal of Trace Elements in Experimental Medicine, no. 12 (May 1999): 71-83,
https://doi.org/10.1002/(SICI)1520-670X(1999)12:2<71::AID-JTRA4>3.0.CO;2-8.

Kondo, Tomoo, Mikiya Kishi, Takashi Fushimi, Shinobu Ugajin, and Takayuki Kaga.
"Vinegar Intake Reduces Body Weight, Body Fat Mass, and Serum Triglyceride Levels in Obese
Japanese Subjects." *Bioscience, Biotechnology, and Biochemistry* 73, no. 8 (August 2009):
1837-1843, https://doi.org/10.1271/bbb.90231.

Mayo Clinic. "Low Carb Diet: Can It Help You Lose Weight?" Accessed March 18, 2019.
https://www.mayoclinic.org/healthy-lifestyle/weight-loss/in-depth/low-carb-diet/
art-20045831.

Momtazi-Borojeni, Amir Abbas, Seyed-Alireza Esmaeili, Elham Abdollahi, Amirhossein Sahebkar.
"A Review on the Pharmacology and Toxicology of Steviol Glycosides Extracted from Stevia
rebaudiana." *Current Pharmaceutical Design* 23, no. 11 2017: 1616-1622,
https://doi.org/10.2174/1381612822666161021142835.

Monterey Bay Aquarium. "Seafood Watch: Shrimp." Accessed April 11, 2019.
https://www.seafoodwatch.org/seafood-recommendations/groups/
shrimp?q=shrimpandt=shrimp.

Noakes, Timothy D. and Johann Windt. "Evidence That Supports the Prescription of Low-
Carbohydrate High-Fat Diets: A Narrative Review." *British Journal of Sports Medicine* 51,
no. 2 (2017): 133-139.

Pearlman, Michelle, Jon Obert, Lisa Casey. "The Association Between Artificial Sweeteners and
Obesity." *Current Gastroenterology Reports* 19, no. 64,
https://doi.org/10.1007/s11894-017-0602-9.

Tey, Siew Ling, Nurhazwani Salleh, Jeya Henry, Ciaran G. Forde. "Effects of Aspartame-,
    Monk Fruit-, Stevia- and Sucrose-Sweetened Beverages on Postprandial Glucose,
    Insulin and Energy Intake." *International Journal of Obesity* 41, no. 3: 450-457,
    https://doi.org/10.1038/ijo.2016.225.

Valenzuela Mencía, Javier, Rafael Fernández Castillo, María Begoña Martos Cabrera,
    José Luis-Gómez-Urquiza, Luis Albendín Garcia, and Guillermo Arturo Cañadas de la Fuente.
    "Diets Low in Carbohydrates for Type 2 Diabetics. Systematic Review." *Nutrición Hospitalaria* 34,
    no. 1: 224-234, https://doi.org/10.20960/nh.999.

Zinn, Caryn, Julia McPhee, Nigel Harris, Micalla Williden, Kate Prendergast, and Grant
    Schofield. "A 12-Week Low-Carbohydrate, High-Fat Diet Improves Metabolic Health Out-
    comes over a Control Diet in a Randomised Controlled Trial with Overweight Defence Force
    Personnel." *Applied Physiology, Nutrition, and Metabolism* 42, no. 11 (2017): 1158-1164,
    https://doi.org/10.1139/apnm-2017-0260.

Index

Acknowledgments

I am incredibly grateful to the team of editors and designers at Callisto Media for their insight into what makes books awesome. I really have learned so much about writing a book from their knowledge and guidance.

Thank you to my kids, Brad and Cole, for your willingness to try all kinds of foods in the kitchen.

Thank you to my husband for pushing me to find creative alternatives to meat. I have learned so much about vegetarian cooking thanks to you.

A final thanks to the scientific community for its research, which continues to illuminate what it means to eat healthfully. I am constantly inspired to try new things, cook with new ingredients, and share what I've learned with others.

About the Author

Pamela Ellgen is the author of more than a dozen cookbooks, including the bestselling *5-Ingredient College Cookbook*, *The Gluten-Free Cookbook for Families*, and *The Low-Carb Cookbook and Weight Loss Plan*. Her work has been featured in *Outside* magazine, *TODAY Food*, *Healthline*, *Huffington Post*, *Edible Phoenix*, *Darling*, and *The Portland Tribune*. Pamela lives in Santa Barbara, California, with her husband and two sons.

CPSIA information can be obtained
at www.ICGtesting.com
Printed in the USA
BVHW060255010819
554793BV00001B/1

9 781641 525077